SECRETS OF SUCCESS AT WORK

50 Techniques to Excel

Nigel Cumberland

SECRETS OF
SUCCESS AT WORK

50 Techniques to Excel

Nigel Cumberland

Also available as an ebook

CONTENTS

This SECRETS book contains a number of special textual features that have been developed to help you navigate the chapters quickly and easily. Throughout the book, you will find these indicated by the following icons.

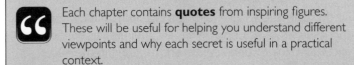 Each chapter contains **quotes** from inspiring figures. These will be useful for helping you understand different viewpoints and why each secret is useful in a practical context.

Also included in each chapter are three **strategies** that outline the ways you can put this secret into practice.

The **putting it all together** box at the end of each chapter provides a summary of each chapter, and a quick way into the core concepts of each secret.

You'll also see a **chapter ribbon** down the right-hand side of each right-hand page, to help you mark your progress through the book and to make it easy to refer back to a particular chapter you found useful or inspiring.

12
13
(14)
15

INTRODUCTION

❝ *'Allow yourself to be inspired. Allow yourself to succeed. Dare to excel.'* Vince Dente

What do really successful working professionals know and do that the rest of us don't? What are their secret recipes for success? Think of people who are excelling in their own work and careers. Who comes to mind? Perhaps you think of a particular colleague, an ex-boss, your father, or a well-known personality such as Jack Welch, Albert Einstein, J. K. Rowling or Steve Jobs. In what ways have such role models been so successful in their work? What they have done that others might have failed to do as well?

No matter what your profession, you can be a success in your work and excel in your job. The 'thousand dollar question' is how can you make this happen? The answers are to be found within this book's 50 secrets.

Today, virtually everybody works in some kind of job or career and on average we spend between 50 per cent and as much as 90 per cent of our waking day at work. As a result, being successful in our work closely equates with having a successful life, with the latter not normally being possible if we are failing to excel in our work life. This makes it imperative that, if you are seeking to have a great life, you must be ready to put in the effort to excel in your work.

The nature of work in the 21st century is also rapidly evolving: the days of having a 'job for life' are a thing of the past and very few of us will spend our lives working in only one organization in the same role and in the same location. Today we might work from home or share a workstation with colleagues, we might have bosses and colleagues based in other locations who we have only ever met online in video conferences, many of us work flexi-time and, in this world of information overload and 24/7 communications, we find ourselves feeling compelled to work all the time. At work we are all increasingly under pressure to perform well and to work harder, and simply being average or satisfactory is not enough as organizations regularly seek cost and efficiency savings through downsizing their workforces and laying off staff. The end result is that we are all expected to do and to achieve more in less time with fewer colleagues and resources to help us.

With the exception of those who give their time on a voluntary or pro bono basis, we all work in order to be paid some kind of income or remuneration and, in return for such money, we are expected to perform well. Our employers expect us to try to succeed in our work and, if we fail to do so, we might lose our job or miss out on salary increases or promotion opportunities. For many of us, not trying to succeed is simply not an option.

All of these workplace changes have meant that the range of skills required to succeed is similarly changing and evolving. In the past it was often enough simply to arrive at work on time, to do exactly what you were told and to be willing to work overtime when needed. Today's working life is more demanding and complicated and to succeed we need a varied toolbox filled with various skills, knowledge and behaviours. The range and number of possible careers and job professions have grown exponentially in recent years; just think of the roles that never existed 10 or 20 years ago, such as those related to information technology, the Internet, biotechnology and the environment.

Each job role or profession might require some specific and unique technical skills but, fortunately, no matter what kind of work you do, the required non-technical people or soft skills are similar across all professions and careers and can be learned and mastered.

In addition to money, we all work for a range of other reasons, and understanding your own reasons or motivations for working can help you to determine how you can optimally succeed in the workplace. Some people work in order to connect with other people, others seek the intellectual stimulation offered by their work, some love to travel in their job, others love being a boss while some simply like doing good work and being acknowledged for this.

This book's secrets are invaluable for everyone who is currently working or who is wishing to enter the workforce. Each reader will relate to each secret and the lists of strategies in different ways, depending on their own experiences and type of career. For those who have recently entered the workforce, so much of this book will seem new and you may need to experiment in applying the secrets to learn which ones are most applicable to your own journey towards work success. For those with a few years of work experience under their belt, this book can help to show you what you have been doing well already while also teaching you what you might have been forgetting to do or were doing incorrectly.

What really constitutes success at work? Excelling in a job can mean different things to each of us and each would define success slightly differently. However, after giving career coaching to hundreds of people over the years, I have learned that work success can be viewed in five different ways:

1. **Being liked and valued by your boss and colleagues** – This requires a broad range of skills and behaviours including emotional intelligence, listening, coaching and integrity.
2. **Achieving and hopefully exceeding your goals** – You will never be viewed as successful if you do not achieve the goals, targets and expectations set by your employer.
3. **Having a career future** – This can be evidenced through you being promoted and having a positive career future while at the same time minimizing the chances of you being laid off or fired.
4. **Doing meaningful and enjoyable work** – Being successful doing work that you do not enjoy or find meaningful is a struggle. It is like being asked to smile when you are not happy.
5. **Avoiding stress and burn-out** – How can anyone claim to be achieving work success if they are letting their working day cause them stress, leaving them drained and burnt out?

These five aspects of work success are what this book's 50 secrets are intended to help you achieve.

When we are young, we might be willing to focus on only the first two or three aspects – working hard to achieve any goals given to you by your boss while also keeping an eye out for the next promotion. Such a person might be working long hours 'burning the midnight oil' and may not enjoy most of what they have to do at work. I would call this an example of partial excelling at work and few, if any, of us could sustain this kind of working life during our entire careers. Such a person's lack of meaning in their work and probable high stress level and chance of burn-out will eventually affect their ability to achieve their performance targets and goals while also reducing the chances of any further career growth and promotions. Success at work must be sustainable and it must not come at a price that you will later regret having paid. After all, it is no good pleasing your boss while you burn out and subsequently need to take lots of sick leave – I would call that a short-lived 'excelling'. This book's 50 secrets aim to share how to achieve a balanced success in the workplace so that you continually excel in your career.

The 50 secrets cover all aspects of possible work success and, when combined together, they will enable you to excel and succeed in whatever jobs or careers you choose to be in. Treat this book as your personal toolbox containing the full range of optimal skills, behaviours and activities that you can draw upon in the right amounts and at the right moments to ensure that you succeed in all aspects of your working life and career. You may find you use some of the tools very often; others you may rarely need to pick up at all. In fact, it would be impossible and frankly absurd to practise all 50 secrets at the same time. There is a time and a place for each of the secrets – for example, there will be times when you must be patient, other times when it is ideal for you to work alone very quickly, while in the next moment you might need to coach a colleague by listening carefully to their issues.

Other people can help you succeed in your work and career, but at the end of the day you are the one in charge of your own life and career and it is up to you to decide how much you wish to succeed and how you will achieve this. Let this book be your guide to professional success and, as you work your way through it, set yourself goals for how you will implement and practise those 'secrets of success at work' that are important to help you to achieve work success, today and in the future. With practice over time, these secrets will become your habits.

Good luck as you embark on your journey to work success. Have the confidence and courage to do what you need to do, taking as your support the words of the poet William Henley:

> *'I am the master of my fate: I am the captain of my soul.'*

Work with your dreams and passions

> 'You are never given a dream without also being given the power to make it true.' Richard Bach

> 'There is no greater gift you can give or receive than to honor your calling. It's why you were born. And how you become most truly alive.' Oprah Winfrey

> 'The secret of joy in work is contained in one word – excellence. To know how to do something well is to enjoy it.' Pearl S. Buck

> 'The only thing that stands between a man and what he really wants from life is often merely the will to try it and the faith to believe that it is possible.' Richard Devos

> 'A musician must make his music, an artist must paint, a poet must write if he is to ultimately be at peace with himself.' Abraham Maslow

During our adult lives we normally spend over half of our day working – working in jobs that we may find boring, fun, difficult, stressful, tiring, exciting, monotonous or relaxing. I coach and train hundreds of people and rarely meet anybody who can tell me that they love their work and are being really successful in their job or career. When I do meet such a person, I like to explore why they feel so contented and successful. In all cases, almost without exception, such people tell me that their work involves things that they love to do, with many telling me that this is their dream job or that they have found their destiny or perfect career.

How can you hope to be truly happy and successful in your work if you are not doing something that you love and find meaningful? I have met accountants who hate numbers, chefs who do not enjoy food and even an airline pilot who has never really enjoyed flying. The pilot told me that, as a child, he dreamed of being a journalist and throughout his life he has enjoyed writing and keeping a diary. When asked why he chose to become a pilot, he shared that his father and uncle were pilots and they encouraged him to follow their career paths. He was not being very successful and ambitious as a pilot and in his airline he was the oldest pilot not to have yet become a captain. His heart was not in his flying but rather in his spare-time writing.

When we enjoy what we are doing, we are happy to learn and explore how to do our work better and we tend to receive more positive feedback and praise which, in turn, tends to make us even happier in our work. It is quite simply easier to succeed at something we enjoy doing than at something we do not – if only because we are more willing and motivated to invest the effort and hard work to do such work better. In your working life, what can you say that you really loved doing and were great at?

RECALL YOUR CHILDHOOD DREAMS

It might sound unusual or even a little corny, but the most contented adults I meet are those whose jobs are made up of activities and tasks that they loved doing as children. There is William who loved playing with guns and is now a Major in the British Army, or Yasmine who spent her youth writing stories and poems and today works for magazines. From a very young age I used to love exploring the area around my Yorkshire village and I have chosen careers which have involved me living and working in over 20 countries in as many years.

I am not suggesting that working in fields that link to your childhood activities and passions will make you totally happy as an adult, although I would always hope this would be possible. I am, rather, suggesting that, when there is some such alignment, you will find work and career choices more enjoyable, less stressful and more fulfilling. Hopefully you will be in what the famous psychologist Csikszentmihalyi calls 'in the flow'.

Can you remember your time as a child? In order to recall what may have been important for you, try answering the following questions and do seek your parents' and siblings' help if your memories are lacking.

- As a child, what did you enjoy doing? Making things? Writing? Playing outside? Does your current work include any of these activities?
- And what did you dream of becoming when you were an adult? How similar is your current work to those childhood dreams?

DECIDE WHAT YOU ENJOY AND FIND MEANINGFUL

Now that you have recalled your childhood dreams and favourite activities, look at yourself as an adult and ask yourself 'What do I enjoy doing today?' I would hope that your answers would overlap with your list of childhood dreams.

Why not spend some time alone or with your partner exploring what you love and enjoy doing? Make notes and map out questions and thoughts raised by the following questions. If it is helpful, draw a mind map to help you brainstorm the ideas, words and answers that come to mind.

- If money were not a problem, what kind of work would you do? Would you stay in your current job, start your own business or do something quite different?
- What do you enjoy doing in your spare time? What hobbies and activities do you do?
- Which friends' or colleagues' jobs and careers do you look upon with a little envy, where you might feel that you would love their job (and not just because of their high remuneration)?

EVALUATE YOUR CURRENT WORK TO FIND PARTS YOU ENJOY AND ARE GOOD AT

Think through how you spend your typical working day or working week and write down a list of your various job activities. If you have a job description, print out a copy and use this document as a basis to draw up the list of your work activities. Do not list what others think you should do or simply rely upon what your job description says; instead, think through what you actually have to do and choose to do when working. Give approximate percentages to the different kinds of tasks and give some kind of ranking to each part. The ranking might be created as follows:

1. Work that you enjoy
2. Work that you are good at
3. Work that you do not enjoy or find boring.

The table shows an example of a list.

Key activities in role	Approx. % of time	Ranking
Leading project teams	30	Good at and enjoy
Chairing meetings	10	Good at and enjoy
Writing reports	20	Good at and find boring
Carrying out research	30	Do not enjoy
Travelling with my work	Varies	Really enjoy

You could then explore your answers and ask yourself:

- How could I do more of what I enjoy and/or am good at, while doing less of what I do not enjoy, find boring and/or am not good at?
- Would it be possible to stay in my job role with my current employer and make my work more enjoyable and filled with those activities that I am good at?

Putting it all together

The phrase 'follow your dreams' has more relevance and value than many imagine. I moved from being a qualified accountant and Finance Director to eventually become what I love, enjoy and am really successful at: a writer, trainer and executive coach. It is crazy to stay in a job or profession which you do not enjoy or find meaningful. Trying to succeed would be an uphill challenge given your probable lack of interest and motivation.

Take the time to recall your childhood dreams and things that you loved to do and then explore what you enjoy doing today as an adult. Have an honest look at your current job and career to see how well it allows you to be who you really want to be and do what you love.

It is better to struggle at work you really enjoy than to succeed in work you find boring and which fails to excite you.

2 Know and fix your blind spots

> 66 'Knowing yourself is the beginning of all wisdom.' Aristotle

> 66 'It doesn't matter what industry you're in. People have blind spots about where they're weak.' Scott Erker

> 66 'He who knows others is wise; he who knows himself is enlightened.' Lao Tzu

> 66 'Until you make peace with who you are, you'll never be content with what you have.' Doris Mortman

> 66 'Know yourself. Don't accept your dog's admiration as conclusive evidence that you are wonderful.' Ann Landers

Knowing ourselves is one of the most important skills that we must possess if we hope to improve how we work and interact with others. Have you ever looked at others and wished they knew themselves better and could see how they are coming across? You may have heard the following kinds of comments spoken about someone:

- 'If only he knew how much he loves his own voice.'
- 'She thinks that she cares but she never listens to other people.'
- 'He acts like he is a great presenter but people fall asleep when they are listening to him.'
- 'She thinks that everyone loves her but we all find her so obnoxious and cold.'

These are examples of what are called 'blind spots', which can be defined as those parts of a person's personality or behaviour that they fail to recognize in themselves. Such blind spots tend to be areas of potential weakness which others can see and will talk or gossip about. They are normally things that we think we are good at or do well, but where other people have the opposite opinion.

Any aspect of a person's personality and behaviour could be possible blind spots and here are some typical examples that I see when coaching and training people:

What the person thinks	What others see and think
'I am a very optimistic and positive person.'	'He is always moaning and complaining.'
'I think that I am very helpful and like to coach my staff.'	'She never has time for us and always seems to be too busy to come over to our workstations.'

Would you be really comfortable if you remain blind to your weaknesses while your work colleagues can see them and might well be talking behind your back, gossiping and complaining about you? Doesn't it feel better or healthier to know more about yourself than those around you do? In my opinion the answers to both of these questions should be a resounding 'Yes, of course.'

BE READY TO SEEK OUT AND ACCEPT THE TRUTH

We are often in denial and sometimes we are not totally blind to some of our behaviours and thinking but instead we choose to ignore them. To use the old saying, we can often brush things under the carpet. I encourage you to be honest with yourself and to decide not to be in such denial. By pretending that some of your weaknesses do not exist, you risk being seen in an even worse light by acting in a way that is ignorant of your own personality and behaviours.

You might feel that you do not know of any of your blind spots. This might be true but do realize that we know ourselves better than we imagine and it can be quite enlightening if we listen to our gut instincts or intuition. If you really cannot think of any blind spots, try out the next strategy.

OBTAIN FEEDBACK FROM THOSE WITH WHOM YOU WORK AND INTERACT

In your organization, how often do you seek feedback about your work and how you are generally performing? In many companies today, feedback is only given once a year as part of a performance evaluation process and sometimes the feedback is given in the form of a 360-degree feedback survey, where the comments are grouped together without enabling you to know who said what.

To truly succeed at work, I encourage you not simply to rely upon such annual processes but instead to proactively ask those with whom you work for some honest thoughts and ideas in answer to the following kinds of question:

- 'I am keen to understand myself better (in my work and as your colleague) and would like to ask a big favour of you – would you be willing to give me your opinion about my strengths and also areas for improvement – for example, about how I communicate and work with you and our colleagues?'
- 'Is there anything which particularly annoys you about my personality and how I act and behave at work?'
- 'If there were one thing I could learn and/or do better, what might that be?'

Stress that any comments or feedback will be kept in confidence and that you will not be upset or negative with that person but will instead be very grateful for their willingness and courage to be so open and honest. Realize that people are not used to being asked such frank questions and may feel uncomfortable saying negative things about you. Respect their decision if they decline to say very much and perhaps revisit the topic later when they have had time to get used to your desire to know the truths about yourself.

Recognize that other people may be intentionally or unintentionally biased and what they share with you may not be totally true. There is a saying that we see our own faults in others; perhaps, when someone says that you are too secretive or noisy at work, it might be that they themselves have such weaknesses which they are projecting on to you. Use your common sense and seek others' opinions to obtain a balanced view of your areas for improvement.

WORK TO OVERCOME YOUR BLIND SPOTS

It is not enough to learn from others about some of your previously unknown weaknesses. If a colleague shares with you that you do not listen enough, or that you become angry in meetings too easily or that your emails are always too long and unclear, be ready to act upon their advice and to work to improve in those areas.

It can seem daunting to have to face weaknesses and then to have to work on them. Why not choose the easiest one first – the so-called 'low-hanging fruit' – and work on it for a while? I would advise you to keep seeking feedback from those you trust, asking them if they can see any positive changes or improvement in particular areas. You can learn more about the importance of seeking feedback in Chapter 43.

Putting it all together

After reading this chapter, I do hope that the five quotes at the chapter's start now resonate with you and that you can feel the importance of knowing yourself – warts and all, to use an English saying. There is no way that you can ever be successful at work on a sustained, ongoing basis if you remain blind to areas where you need to grow and improve. Nobody is saying that you must become perfect overnight, but at least aim to know yourself really well.

I realize that seeking the help of others – including asking for feedback in the second strategy above – will take great courage, and you will need to make sure that you do not allow yourself to get too upset at what you hear.

As you work through the remainder of this book, we will explore all kinds of skills, behaviours and actions that you can employ to help you achieve work and career success. In doing so, you will come across many possible areas of blind spots, which you will now be able to understand and overcome.

3 Work with your strengths and weaknesses

❝ *'Success is achieved by developing our strengths, not by eliminating our weaknesses.'* Marilyn vos Savant

❝ *'Play to your strengths.'* J. K. Rowling (*Harry Potter and the Goblet of Fire*)

❝ *'I actually think one of my strengths is my storytelling.'* Quentin Tarantino

❝ *'Life is very interesting… in the end, some of your greatest pains become your greatest strengths.'* Drew Barrymore

❝ *'Build upon strengths, and weaknesses will gradually take care of themselves.'* Joyce C. Lock

We all possess a range of skills, personality traits and behaviours which are often grouped together and called competencies. If you have followed the advice in the previous chapter on blind spots, you should now have a better awareness of your own full range of competencies.

Nobody in the workplace is a perfect employee who has the exact combination of strengths needed without having any weaknesses. Somebody might have the ideal communication, decision-making and delegation skills while at the same time being too impatient and not being numbers-oriented enough. Even if someone today seems to have the perfect combination of strengths, they might find that an aspect of their personality that used to be a strength might be a weakness once they are promoted or moved to another role. An example of this might be a salesman who is self-centred and focused only on his own sales who might need to tone down such strengths if he or she were to be promoted to a sales manager position.

Are you using and playing to all of your strengths in your current job and career? Are any of your weaker skills and behaviours interfering with your ability to do your job well? In an ideal world, everyone's work should make use of their strengths while not being affected by any of their weaknesses, but sadly this is rarely the case.

If you have worked through Chapter 1, you will have an idea of how closely your current work aligns to your dream or ideal work. The closer the alignment, the higher the probability that your work is using your strengths and is not being influenced by your weaknesses.

KNOW YOUR STRENGTHS AND WEAKNESSES

A common job interview question is to ask about a candidate's strengths and weaknesses. Have you ever been asked this kind of question before?

It is really helpful to know and understand all of your strengths and weaknesses. Make a list of them now – in buckets or sub-categories, such as work experience, knowledge/education, skills and behaviours. If you have worked through the previous chapter on blind spots, you will hopefully have a good idea of what they are.

Being able to understand and list your areas of work experience, hard skills, knowledge and education should be relatively straightforward. Where you may have more difficulty is in listing your soft skills, personality traits and behaviours. Consider using an assessment tool to help you rank the relative strengths of your personality-related attributes. Such tools can be found on the Internet and are either free or relatively inexpensive. Examples include the Harrison assessment, the Hogan Instrument, the DISC assessment and the MBTI profiling tool.

EXPLORE HOW YOU CAN BETTER USE YOUR STRENGTHS IN YOUR CURRENT JOB ROLE

I once knew an accountant who did not enjoy working with numbers but really enjoyed other aspects of her job, including helping and training her team. Sadly, because she was not so comfortable with numbers, she made one mistake too many when creating important spreadsheets and was eventually fired. Afterwards, she did admit to me that she has now pursued her dream job of working in training and human resources, where I am happy to report that she plays to her strengths and does not need to rely upon her areas of weakness. Are you truly playing to your strengths in your work?

This idea of playing to your strengths and how to make others, including your boss, truly aware of the benefits of your strengths is a very important success factor for anyone in the working world. Sit down and list your strengths and explore how they are being used and also recognized in your work. As a rule of thumb, if less than half of your strengths are being used in your current work, you might not be in an optimal job role or profession. Furthermore, if we do not use our strengths, we can feel very frustrated and this can negatively impact upon our work.

PLAN HOW YOU CAN GROW YOUR JOB ROLE AND CAREER TO BETTER USE YOUR STRENGTHS

The accountant I mentioned above waited to be fired before starting to look for work that better used her strengths and relied less upon areas where she didn't naturally excel. If you genuinely and honestly believe that your strengths would be better used in another job role (ideally your dream job), then start planning to move to such a job now. Do not wait until you fail in your current work or become burnt out and stressed by doing work that you are finding hard because it doesn't fit your skill set. Consider seeking the help of a career coach to help you plan any needed change – perhaps you will need to go back to study or move into a new career where you will need to humble yourself by starting at the bottom. These are not easy choices to make and your family and friends might try to talk you out of taking such risky decisions and making such changes, so do be careful from whom you seek advice and support.

Putting it all together

I do hope that this chapter is encouraging you to take an honest look at your various strengths and weaknesses and the degree to which your current work uses your strengths and is possibly being held back by your weaknesses. The next challenge is to decide how you ensure that any future work roles and career choices more optimally use and build on your strengths while requiring less of the areas in which you don't naturally perform as well.

As you work through this book, you might discover skills and behaviours in which you are neither strong nor weak, probably because you may never have used and seen them before. Your challenge will be to decide whether you need to add to your toolkit of strengths. If in doubt, add them, as you never know when a particular skill or ability will be useful.

4 Deliver on your promises and commitments

❝ *'Don't ever promise more than you can deliver, but always deliver more than you promise.'* Lou Holtz

❝ *'Promises are like crying babies in a theater, they should be carried out at once.'* Norman Vincent Peale

❝ *'You've got to deliver on short-range commitments, while you develop a long-range strategy and vision and implement it.'* Jack Welch

❝ *'Losers make promises they often break. Winners make commitments they always keep.'* Denis Waitley

❝ *'He was ever precise in promise-keeping.'* William Shakespeare

Are you a person of your word? Are you careful to promise or commit to only what you can achieve and, in the event that circumstances may make this impossible, do you communicate honestly and as soon as possible with the affected parties?

In a workshop I once asked a group the following question: would you prefer to work with a friend who does not keep their word or an enemy who does? We explored this question and the entire group said that they would prefer to work with enemies they could in some sense trust rather than with friends who may not keep their word and promises. How often have you been let down by others who had agreed or offered to say or do something to help or to support you but who you later discovered had not done as they had promised? Such moments can sometimes be hard to forget, particularly when those people might have lied to you, perhaps saying that they had done something when they had not.

Do you have any colleagues or staff who, over time, you have come to realize rarely achieve or do what they promise or agree to do? Do you keep getting annoyed with them, or do you let it go or, even more interestingly, do you avoid giving them critical and important tasks for fear of them not completing them properly and/or on time? In my executive coaching experience, I find this is quite a common occurrence and it is a key factor which influences productivity within organizations. When a team's boss acts in such a way, you can be sure that the team's levels of motivation and engagement will be negatively affected.

Some people are so keen to please that they will readily agree to, promise and commit to almost anything. Such people never seem to learn from their repeatedly missed deadlines and failing to deliver or do what others have been promised. They are also normally blind to the idea of managing other peoples' expectations and may never warn others that they are behind schedule or unable to do what they had promised.

CARRY OUT AN AUDIT OF YOUR PROMISES AND COMMITMENTS

For the next couple of weeks, keep a journal or notes about all the promises and commitments that you have made and are making. You might be surprised how many times you make formal and informal promises and commitments and, in doing so, give others expectations of what you are going to do. Sometimes even your silence can be taken as agreement to do something, with the other party later claiming: 'But you didn't turn down my request so I assumed you were doing the work!'

PAUSE AND REFLECT BEFORE MAKING NEW PROMISES AND COMMITMENTS

Give yourself time before rushing to respond to requests from your boss, colleagues and other stakeholders at your workplace. Try to be very specific in how you respond when you are asked to promise or commit to do something. If you are not sure whether you can do what is being asked of you, do not simply say, 'I'll try and let you know' because people could assume that this means that you will be doing as they have asked.

I would always encourage you to under-promise from now on – if you think a task will take one week, promise to do it in ten days or two weeks. Let the other party push back and negotiate if necessary. You can then impress them by completing the task in less time than expected.

FOCUS EXTRA ATTENTION ON THOSE PROMISES THAT ARE DIFFICULT TO FULFIL

When I was a finance director, I had an enormous workload and I recall having a regular problem when keeping my promises to read new project plans and report back to people. I always seemed to be late in giving the other party my feedback and they would email or phone to chase me. This created anxiety and tension and I would then feel compelled to rush. After this had happened one too many times, I realized that I was finding it really tedious and boring to review such plans. The solution I arrived at was to ask those with the draft plans to sit down with me and walk me through them and together we would edit the plans.

Your challenge is to discover what, if any, recurring commitment issues you have and how you might operate differently to fulfil them. I once coached a CEO who was always late for meetings because he allowed himself to get distracted. He solved this problem by holding as many future meetings as he could in his own office, which made it much harder for him to be late! Finding such solutions will test your levels of creativity and innovation. You could perhaps sit down with colleagues and discuss those work commitments that you find particularly hard to fulfil and together you might be able to come up with workable solutions.

In having started to read my book, I hope that you are committing and promising (to yourself) to read the whole thing from cover to cover. You may only skim read it and you may move between chapters, but I encourage you to get into the habit of always committing to do what you say you will. In your workplace, no matter whether you are a new employee or an established leader, let your colleagues and team know that, from today onwards, you intend to 'walk your talk' and to try always to do and complete what you commit to do and avoid making any false promises.

You may discover that part of your problem is that you accept too much work and do not say no often enough. Realize that you cannot continue to say yes to everything requested of you. In addition to missing deadlines and annoying your colleagues and stakeholders, your over-promising may cause you stress and anxiety because you will have to deal with people pushing you and complaining about you.

5 Work with trust and integrity

> *'The key is to get to know people and trust them to be who they are. Instead, we trust people to be who we want them to be – and when they're not, we cry.'* David Duchovny

> *'You cannot do everything at once, so find people you trust to help you. And don't be afraid to say no.'* Jane Seymour

> *'Trust is the glue of life. It's the most essential ingredient in effective communication. It's the foundational principle that holds all relationships.'* Stephen Covey

> *'Learning to trust is one of life's most difficult tasks.'* Isaac Watts

> *'Have the courage to say no. Have the courage to face the truth. Do the right thing because it is right. These are the magic keys to living your life with integrity.'* W. Clement Stone

Being a person whom others can trust is one of the most sought-after qualities in the workplace today. So many leaders and their staff have shown in the recent global financial crisis a lack of trust and integrity among themselves and with their clients and other stakeholders. The trust that did exist was a collusive type, whereby people agreed not to whistle-blow on each other about any illegal or unethical actions and behaviours. When I talk about trust in this chapter, I refer to a more positive and altruistic kind, which links to doing things with integrity.

Trust and integrity go hand in hand, with integrity being doing the right thing and trust being the sense that others know that you will do the right thing, again and again and again. It takes time working with colleagues and clients to build up a reputation for being someone of integrity whom others can trust, but such reputations can be damaged or indeed destroyed by one thoughtless or inappropriate act or conversation. Once you lose someone's trust, everything changes – they might forgive you but they will never forget.

In my experience, one of the main reasons why a boss would support a member of his team being given a promotion is because of his trust in that individual – organizations really value and support people whom they can trust.

Trust is two-way and, in addition to endeavouring to be a person of integrity whom others trust, you should always aim only to work with people of integrity whom you can trust. The end outcome is that you should aspire to work in cultures of trust and integrity.

SPEAK THE TRUTH

Starting today, in any work discussion or communication, observe what you are thinking and communicating. Are you being honest and truthful and, if not, why not? I am not suggesting that you become your organization's primary whistle-blower, raising the lid on untold secrets, but rather I am suggesting that you avoid the multitude of little lies that we speak and act out all the time when we are at work. Examples might include:

- telling your boss that you have read the draft report when you have not
- supporting a business idea when you totally disagree with it
- cheating on your travel expenses
- stealing office stationery
- being late for a meeting and making up a lie about why you were delayed.

In my experience, such lies and deceit could be viewed as small matters, but my concern is with their combined impact on your personality and character. As you continually lie in this way, larger lies might start appearing and you may also begin lying to yourself:

- 'It's okay to steal office stationery because it's not expensive and anyway I'm underpaid.'
- 'Everyone else seems to be late for meetings, so it's okay for me to be late as well.'
- 'I am happy in my job' – when in truth you are crying out inside to change careers.
- Each day you work with colleagues whom you might detest, but you simply smile and pretend that you like them all and even socialize with them.

I also know that, when people allow themselves to work in this way, their personal life becomes similarly infected with small untruths and you might reach a point where you do not even trust yourself and your own thoughts and opinions.

BE READY TO REQUEST INTEGRITY AND TRUTH FROM OTHERS

How often do you ever direct comments or questions like the following to a colleague or to your boss?

- 'Let's be honest about this work problem and discuss all possible solutions.'
- 'Can we share our honest feelings and thoughts about this business plan?'
- 'It's okay if you have not read my draft report. Rather than say you have and make comments, perhaps you could skim read it now and give me your thoughts.'
- 'Could I please ask you to give me honest and truthful feedback about my performance?'

I urge you to say such things – to support and to nudge others to be more honest and truthful in a diplomatic manner. Can you visualize how much healthier the working environment would become? I can assure you it will be.

I have coached individuals who claim that they are not liked and not supported in their work environment if they try to be honest. In response I have encouraged them to ask themselves if they are working in the ideal work environment and, if not, should they find a more ideal place in which to work? I help many organizations all over the world and can confirm that there are many work environments where honesty and integrity are valued, recognized and rewarded.

DO NOT LIE TO YOURSELF

Never lie to yourself and spend each day in denial about some important aspects of your personality and working style:

- If you do not like some of your work or your job, then admit it to yourself and decide either to stay or to plan how you might make a change.
- If your work is not using your strengths, do not pretend otherwise to yourself.
- If you find it very difficult working under your boss or with certain colleagues, be honest with yourself and think through how you might respond. Do you share your concerns, or do you keep quiet? Do you seek to move departments or do you plan to find a new job?

You do not have to communicate all of your true opinions and feelings to other people – being diplomatic is an important skill to possess!

Putting it all together

Aim to work in an organization where honesty, truth and integrity are valued and admired. If you feel that your current organization is not ideal in this way, do not lose heart but try to be honest and trustworthy yourself. What can go wrong? You get fired for being such a person? It is far better to be fired for being honest than to be fired for lying. However, I do hope that you are never put in such a difficult situation.

Remember that it starts with small things, avoiding those little untruths that so easily creep into our working day. When you are late for a meeting, be honest and avoid fictitious excuses. When you have not finished reading a report, avoid pretending that you have. When you feel that your annual performance evaluation by your boss is not fair, say so (diplomatically).

And, finally, remember above all to be true to yourself. It is fine to act and to pretend that something is okay, but always admit the truth to yourself.

These things are, to paraphrase Clement Stone from the start of this chapter, the 'magic keys' to having a successful working life.

6 Work positively and have fun

> 'Positive thinking will let you do everything better than negative thinking will.' Zig Ziglar

> 'In order to carry a positive action we must develop here a positive vision.' Dalai Lama

> 'People rarely succeed unless they have fun in what they are doing.' Dale Carnegie

> 'I think we're having fun. I think our customers really like our products. And we're always trying to do better.' Steve Jobs

> 'Keep your face always toward the sun – and shadows will fall behind you.' Walt Whitman

I have discovered a simple truth: people prefer working with fun and positive colleagues and they typically will avoid spending time with anyone who is negative, moody and too serious.

The recently deceased Apple co-founder Steve Jobs often spoke about his company's success being built upon staff having fun, doing what they love and being positive. So many other successful people say the same thing and all seem to enjoy getting up in the mornings and going to work. I suspect that they do not suffer from 'Monday morning blues'. Do you look forward to going to work each day? And, once you are at work, do you enjoy what you do and do you have fun in a positive work environment?

Can you really be successful at work while at the same time being and feeling negative, unhappy and bored? People have responded that, in some work environments, it is viewed as inappropriate to act in a fun and happy way. I do hope that your work environment is optimal for you and that you are able to work in as positive and fun a way as you wish. I need to be in a positive and fun environment and only then am I able to express myself naturally.

Do you have a fun and positive mindset and personality, and do you work with a positive attitude, acting as if the 'glass is half full' as you spend time working? Do your colleagues enjoy working with and communicating with you? Growing numbers of studies and theories, including in the fields of positive psychology, all arrive at a similar conclusion, tying a person's level of positive thinking and attitude to success in the workplace. Quite simply, people prefer to hire, to work with and to promote colleagues and staff who are fun to work with and who have a positive attitude. After many years of working with all kinds of individuals, I am convinced that we can all learn to be positive and fun in the workplace. I don't believe that such qualities are things that we are born with or without, which are then set in stone. We can create the reality that we want if we put our mind to it.

FAKE IT UNTIL YOU MAKE IT

Are you a serious person at work – the kind of person who rarely seems to smile or laugh and who never tells a funny story or joke? And do you feel that you are not capable of changing your habits?

The best advice for you is to act positively, and be fun and happy even if it is not natural for you to do and even if you might be uncomfortable. It is often stated that smiling uses fewer muscles than frowning and I know from having helped many people that the more that you practise being positive, the easier it becomes – and it does become a habit.

PAUSE BEFORE REACTING AND THEN REACT POSITIVELY

Throughout our working day we are having to react – react to emails, to people speaking with us, to discussions in meetings, to gossip heard by the water cooler, to accusations made by a colleague, to urgent requests from our boss… The list can seem endless. The secret to success is to ensure that, each time you need to respond, you do so in the most positive and thoughtful way possible. Do not rush to react in a harsh and negative way but, instead, try to put on a smile and see the best in any situation. My mother always used to tell me to 'count to ten' before reacting when someone had annoyed me, and this was probably one of the best pieces of advice I ever received because it has become a great habit. People who heed this advice become used to spending a second or two reflecting before speaking, even when they are in a very rushed situation.

Try pausing. If you would like a visual prompt card, then I would suggest that you write 'STOP & WAIT' on a card and that you carry it with you and place it in front of you on the table in meetings. These two words stand for the following:

S = Stop   **W** = Why

T = Think   **A** = Am

O = (Review) Options   **I** = I

P = Proceed   **T** = Talking?

Furthermore, if anyone sees your cards and asks you what they are for, they will enjoy hearing what the two sets of letters mean and it might help them to reflect on how reactive they might be too.

CREATE FUN MOMENTS AT WORK

Some of you might recall the American doctor called Patch Adams whose life story was turned into a film. Patch became famous for being funny and clowning about in front of very ill and sometimes terminally ill patients. This upset other doctors and hospital staff but, over time, they came to understand and to accept that being so positive and fun really did lift the spirits of the patients, their families and also the hospital staff and it seemed to play a part in easing the patients' suffering and pain.

In a less dramatic way, by being positive and fun, you can help your colleagues to relieve their stress and anxiety and make coming to work slightly less of a burden than is for so many.

Starting from today, resolve to make others happy and relaxed by creating some fun, light-hearted moments. For example, be ready to break the tension in a meeting that seems to be going on for too long – but do so appropriately and do not become too irreverent, for instance by cracking one joke too many in a business meeting. Perhaps your department has become lazy about celebrating people's birthdays? When your next colleague has a birthday, have a cake and perhaps ask people to share a fun memory or story about the colleague whose birthday it is. Such fun moments are thoughtful and memorable and are what your colleagues will share when they go home, rather than moaning about the work problems they are facing.

Putting it all together

There is absolutely no way that you can have sustained success at work if, in the eyes of your colleagues, peers and staff, you are someone who is not positive and no fun to work with. People might put up with you, but they are unlikely to support promoting you or to put up their hands to offer to work with you. If you are not sure how positive and fun you appear, ask some of your trusted colleagues for their opinion. No one expects you to become the office clown or jester, but try to be to more easy-going and positive than most people and this will make you more popular and successful in winning people over.

The three strategies above are all interlinked and can be summarized simply: act in a more positive and fun way in the workplace and it will eventually become a habit. You could always start in small ways, such as by smiling a little more, by saying well done to your colleagues or by bringing some doughnuts into work for your staff even when there is no special reason.

7　Work patiently and persistently

> 'Patience, persistence and perspiration make an unbeatable combination for success.' Napoleon Hill

> 'How poor are they that have not patience! What wound did ever heal but by degrees?' William Shakespeare

> 'The key to everything is patience. You get the chicken by hatching the egg, not by smashing it.' Arnold H. Glasgow

> 'One moment of patience may ward off great disaster. One moment of impatience may ruin a whole life.' Chinese proverb

> 'It's not that I'm so smart, it's just that I stay with problems longer.' Albert Einstein

You have now reached Secret 7 and I wonder if you will have the patience and persistence to read the entire book. More importantly, will you devote the time to actually practise many of the suggested strategies?

We live in a world where so many things are instantly available and I realize that many people seem to want work and career success today and fail to appreciate that so many aspects of work success take time. How can you claim to be doing a good job when you might not yet have had enough time to learn how to do your work well? In some professions this takes weeks; in others it might take years.

Patience is about learning to accept that you need to give yourself time to do well what you have been employed to do. I challenge you to be patient and not to expect overnight recognition and success, and to allow time for your work to be recognized. We must not let stress, pressure or anxieties make us too impatient.

It is never easy to know when to continue with something and when to change or give up. But as a general rule, if in doubt, be persistent and stay with that work or task a little longer while you explore your options. Do not become someone who regrets leaving a job or resigning from a company, who realizes with hindsight that they should have stayed longer and stuck it out. Beware of believing that the grass is always greener elsewhere and allowing yourself to job-hop.

LEARN TO WAIT

Patience can be learned and I realize that we develop different levels of patience when we are children. Then, as we enter the working world, we get into the habit of being either more patient or more impatient than other people. I also know that being impatient with other people is a sign that we are also being impatient with different aspects of ourselves.

How often do you become impatient either with yourself or with your colleagues? Watch yourself for a day and observe both what you think and what you do. Explore when you might be acting hastily and impatiently and also ask one or more of your colleagues what they think. Practise being more patient in situations where you realize that giving something or someone a little more time can be a positive thing.

As an example, I recently coached a leader who would read and reply to all his emails far too quickly. This would often upset his colleagues, particularly when the leader's replies were inappropriate, for instance unnecessarily negative or abrasive. I also learned that this leader was equally impatient with himself. I encouraged him to read emails more slowly and, if he was replying to one, to read the message twice, ensuring that he scrolled down in order to read the entire email, and only then to reply.

Find an activity that you might be impatient doing or a person who you might be impatient with and practise slowing down and taking your time. Doing this repeatedly will help you develop this habit.

PRACTISE BEING PERSISTENT

We all give up on things and people, with some of us doing it sooner and more often than others. I often have salesmen call me to sell their products and services. After I tell them that I have no interest, some simply put the phone down, some keep chatting and others call me back later, still trying to elicit interest from me. I used to coach people in job-hunting skills and the hardest skill to teach many was to learn to persist and not to give up in the face of many potential employers either rejecting or simply ignoring the job-hunters' applications, emails and phone calls.

If something is important to you, then persist in obtaining it. As with the strategy above, think about key aspects of your job and ask yourself, 'When am I giving up too easily?' and identify tasks with which you will consciously persist more than you would have in the past. It might be in looking for a great engineer to hire, trying to meet with a potential client or solving some difficult work problem.

TEACH A COLLEAGUE PATIENCE AND PERSISTENCE

It is easier to work with more patience and persistence if those you work around also wish to do the same thing.

Within your team or department, who might you encourage to act and to work with a little more patience or persistence? Who seems to rush too much or to give up too easily? In what ways might you encourage that person to see the value of being a little more patient or persistent? They may not wish to be lectured to (after all, who does?) but you could make some helpful suggestions, such as:

- 'I can see that you are getting a little bit frustrated with the other department being slow to pass you the

information. Maybe you need to go over there to see how you can help them to complete the work?'
- 'I realize that you feel like giving up on this employee who is performing poorly, but in what ways could you give him another chance?'

Sometimes just a few small words of encouragement or simple suggestions can be enough to persuade someone to be a little more patient or persistent than they would otherwise have been.

Putting it all together

We live in a material world of instant gratification and where things have to be done now and we no longer have to wait for much. To ensure that we have work success, we need to push ourselves to act with more patience and persistence than we might naturally choose to exhibit. I often interview graduates for job openings and am surprised how often they ask how soon they can become managers or have a company car or have their first overseas business trips. Ambition is admirable but such questions also suggest that these young people might lack the optimal levels of patience and persistence that would help them succeed in the workplace.

No matter how busy you are or how urgent your many work tasks are, remember that there will be times when you need to wait and be patient. Another way to view this is to become aware when you might be acting too impatiently with yourself or with other people. When it is optimal to be patient, you will discover that you will also need to be persistent and not get frustrated if you cannot easily or quickly complete a task. Patience and persistence come more naturally to people with calmer personalities; for those people who are always wanting action and to do things, it may take more effort to acquire these habits. It can also be quite challenging trying to encourage colleagues to show a little more patience or persistence in their own work.

8 Work smart

> 'Your ability to discipline yourself to set clear goals, and then to work toward them every day, will do more to guarantee your success than any other single factor.' Brian Tracy

> 'Working hard becomes a habit, a serious kind of fun. You get self-satisfaction from pushing yourself to the limit, knowing that all the effort is going to pay off.' Mary Lou Retton

> 'You have to learn the rules of the game. And then you have to play better than anyone else.' Albert Einstein

> 'The average person puts only 25 per cent of his energy and ability into his work.' Andrew Carnegie

> 'Talent is never enough. With few exceptions the best players are the hardest workers.' Magic Johnson

How often do you stay working in your office in the evenings? So many people spend long hours at work but often they are not being very productive or, to use different terminology, they are not working very smart. I am sure that you have heard the saying that it is quality not quantity that matters, and this is very true in terms of your time spent at work.

Anyone can spend more time than their colleagues at work and become viewed as a workaholic. Working intelligently with a strong ethic and being a workaholic are not the same thing. We all typically have too much to do in our jobs, with long to-do lists and all kinds of goals to achieve. Your challenge is to complete work that is important and be seen to be on top of your job but without having to work late into the evenings or at weekends. This is not an easy task.

The secret is to use your brain and your time wisely, making sensible choices about what you focus on and for how long and when. Working smart can also involve maximizing how you share your work with others – delegating tasks to others where appropriate and possible.

Working smart becomes easier to achieve if you genuinely wish to have a work–life balance and to leave work at or close to the official end of the working day – for example, leaving work at 6 p.m. in a company where the official end of the day is 5 p.m. or 5.30 p.m., rather than regularly leaving after 8 p.m. and never having time with your young children. I have known so many fathers, and some mothers, who would leave home in the mornings when it is still dark and arrive home in the evenings when their children are sleeping. What is smart about that?

We all need to impress and to work hard in our jobs, particularly when we feel that our job may not be secure, but this should not be at the price of working in ways that could be viewed as inefficient and leave you stuck in the office.

AIM TO DO THE RIGHT THINGS WELL

There is a definition of excellence which is doing those tasks which are the right or needed ones, and doing these tasks in the optimal and most efficient ways. In other words, excellence is doing the right things and doing them in the right way. In an ideal world, a truly successful person at work would only do this and avoid making either of the following two errors or mistakes:

- doing the right tasks but in the wrong way
- doing correctly the wrong tasks.

When you observe colleagues, particularly those who are not performing well, you will notice that each is guilty of one or both of these mistakes. To ensure that you never fall into the same trap, always be ready to ask yourself two questions:

- Is this task or goal what really needs to be done or achieved?
- Is this the best way of doing or achieving this task?

DO NOT WASTE TIME ON EASY BUT UNIMPORTANT TASKS

Watch how you spend your working day. Are you spending longer than needed in meetings that you do not really have to attend and where you can see little value in being present? Are you working on simple tasks that might be taking up too much time and that you might consider delegating or outsourcing? Perhaps you are in the habit of taking long lunch breaks and coffee breaks and then at the end of the day feel compelled to stay on at work to complete urgent tasks. If this is the case, might you have shorter breaks?

It is surprising how we get into habits that become potentially time-wasting. It can sometimes be hard to see your own habits and patterns, and you might ask a close colleague for their opinions about how you seem to be spending your day and where you might be unproductive.

People may share with you that taking your time on certain non-essential tasks can provide great opportunities for valuable networking and relationship building. This can often be the case when attending meetings, for example, but in such cases you must weigh up whether doing something else might not be a better use of your time.

ENCOURAGE THOSE AROUND YOU TO WORK 'SMART'

Are you surrounded by colleagues who seem always to work long hours? Perhaps your entire department or floor all seem to copy each other and leave the office a few hours later than the official working hours. Do your colleagues complain that they have too much to do and never have enough time?

You can win favour with colleagues by sitting down with them to explore how they might work more effectively and smartly. You can even offer to observe how they spend their working day and to offer your thoughts. Most importantly, you could encourage your colleagues to try to leave work on time. I used to challenge my colleagues to aim to be home at least three times a week in time to have dinner with their partner and/or children.

What do you do if it is your boss that you feel is in most need of guidance on how to work more smartly? I used to have a boss who had no children and he would normally stay in the office until 9 p.m. each night (in a company where most staff left at around 6 p.m.). He would happily allow meetings to drag on and never seemed to respect other people's time and workloads. The worst thing was that he would make sarcastic comments to any of us who chose to leave the office before him. After working like this for over a year, I decided that enough was enough and I asked to have a word with him. I shared my observations and frustrations and asked if he would respect my need to balance my home and work life and to be able to work a very productive day and to leave the office at or close to 6 p.m. What was his response? He admitted that nobody had ever pointed this out to him before and he actually apologized. From that day forward he stopped making staff feel bad about leaving the office before him and he tried to ensure that his team could be as productive as possible during normal working hours.

Putting it all together

You cannot achieve your work goals and claim to be successful if you spend too many hours at work and spend many of those hours working unproductively or in some way inefficiently.

By focusing on trying to 'work smart' and also encouraging colleagues to work in smarter ways and to use their time more productively, you can make yourself more productive with a better work–life balance while helping those with whom you work to achieve the same.

Before starting to work through this chapter's three strategies, set yourself what I will call a 'statement of intent' that states what you wish to achieve. Your wording might be something like this:

I wish to work as productively and efficiently as possible during the normal working day, so that I can leave work at a reasonable time and also not feel the need to take work home. I will be as assertive as needed, letting my boss and others know when our expectations differ, for example about when I should leave the office.

I know of a colleague who wrote such a statement and stuck it prominently in his work station for all to see.

Life is too short to spend too long at work or to waste your time while you are at work. There will always be times when you will need to work longer hours than normal or you find that working on a certain task or project was not very productive (often the case with new tasks) – but these should be the exception in your working week, not the norm.

9 Work with empathy

> 'The great gift of human beings is that we have the power of empathy.' Meryl Streep

> 'Be kind whenever possible. It is always possible.' Tenzin Gyatso, 14th Dalai Lama

> 'When you start to develop your powers of empathy and imagination, the whole world opens up to you.' Susan Sarandon

> 'If there is any one secret of success, it lies in the ability to get the other person's point of view and see things from his angle as well as your own.' Henry Ford

> 'The most important trip you may take in life is meeting people halfway.' Henry Boye

Empathy is the skill of being able to sense and to understand what others are experiencing, feeling and thinking. It is about being able to view the world through another person's eyes and to put yourself in their shoes. We all have this skill but for many it does not seem very well developed and used. During my coaching work I am astonished how often I hear comments about people's line managers (or bosses) not realizing or noticing things, such as when one of the team is stressed, tired, overworked, confused, scared of a change or needing to talk.

The working world needs more empathic leaders, staff and colleagues. A high level of empathy will make up for a person's lack of a wide array of other skills and attributes. When surveyed, people tend to agree that they would much prefer working with a strong and demanding boss or colleague who truly cares over an easy-going and undemanding boss who exhibits no empathy. We all need to be recognized and feel valued, and this is unlikely to come from a boss who has little empathy.

Have you ever seen a child who stops running in a race to help a friend who has tripped over? Some people do seem to have been brought up with a higher level of empathy than others exhibit. The great news is that empathy can be learned and acquired by us all and in many ways this is similar to practising being positive and fun, which we covered in an earlier chapter. The challenge is to understand how empathic you already are and adjust your level as needed.

LISTEN TO OTHERS WELL IN A CARING WAY

We are all encouraged to listen to others in the workplace, regardless of whether we are simply an employee or a manager, but being empathic is more than just hearing the words that someone is saying. We need to listen to people, whether they speak to us in person, on the telephone or through an email, and to demonstrate that we have heard what they are saying and meaning. This should involve a combination of the following:

- stopping what you are doing to focus on the other person and, if face to face, looking them in the eye and smiling
- not interrupting the other person and also ensuring that you are present and not letting your mind wander while the other person speaks or while you read a person's email
- pausing before responding to what you hear to give your brain a few seconds to absorb and understand what has been shared
- paraphrasing or summarizing back to the person what you understand they are trying to say – for example, 'So what I am hearing is that…, am I correct?'
- expressing genuine understanding, which, depending on the conversation's contents, might include you responding in any number of ways – for example 'I can understand that this is not easy for you', 'I can see that you will need time

and the support of the department' or 'I can understand that your department must have been working long hours and this cannot be easy for your team.'

You will be surprised how positive the other party will be with you if you demonstrate that you care enough to listen. We all long to be heard and hearing others is an important skill in the workplace.

ASK OTHERS HOW THEY ARE DOING AND COPING

So many people are working with stress and anxiety and we all seem to be overworked and burdened with work. When interviewed, many depressed and suicidal people admit that what they often longed for was someone to ask them how they were doing or how they felt. I think that this applies generally to the workplace – a colleague does not have to be depressed or suicidal but simply a bit overworked and stressed. There may be times when you realize that a colleague is facing a particular challenge or difficulty. Why not try going up to colleagues or team members in these situations and just asking them how things are going and if there is anything you can do to help? Occasionally take a colleague for coffee or meet them for lunch. You could say something to them like, 'We don't seem to speak very much and it would be nice to catch up.'

SUPPORT AND ENCOURAGE YOUR BOSS TO BE EMPATHIC

You may have a boss who is very empathic and caring and who takes time to listen to and understand the issues and challenges you are facing. If you are not so fortunate, you may recognize moments when your boss seems to fail to notice that you or one of your colleagues are facing a particular issue or challenge or feeling especially concerned, worried or anxious about something. At such times it might be appropriate to have a quiet word with your boss to let him or her know.

Some bosses will not 'get it' and, even if prompted, might be unable to understand what they could do to show that they care. Some may watch one of their team or a colleague being caring and empathic and they may not even recognize such behaviour or may see it as being too soft and emotional. With a boss who is failing to show empathy, you can 'bring them to the water, but you cannot force them to drink'. However, seeing you repeatedly act with empathy might eventually begin to rub off on them.

Putting it all together

Empathy is an essential ingredient which will help you to be valued, appreciated and liked by others with whom you work. Empathy in itself is a form of work success but, more importantly, by being empathic, you will have better relationships with your colleagues and all those with whom you work. This in turn ought to make it easier for you to be successful in other ways, many of which are covered in this book. Quite simply, people prefer to work with someone who cares about them, even if there are times when that person will need to push, be demanding or even have to make uncomfortable decisions which affect those around them.

To recap, you should develop and strengthen your own empathy by genuinely listening well and regularly asking others how they are doing. If you are unlucky, you may have an uncaring boss and he or she may even make it hard for you to demonstrate your own empathy and caring. If this is the case, think how you might be able to help your boss become more empathic.

Work with mentors

CC *'A mentor is someone who sees more talent and ability within you than you see in yourself, and helps bring it out of you.'*
Bob Proctor

CC *'I think a role model is a mentor – someone you see on a daily basis, and you learn from them.'* Denzel Washington

CC *'Everyone, no matter how big and strong, could use a little help sometimes. Never be afraid to ask for help when you need it. What are we here for, if not for each other?'* Doe Zantamata

CC *'All you need to do to receive guidance is to ask for it and then listen.'* Sanaya Roman

CC *'When you see a worthy person, endeavor to emulate him. When you see an unworthy person, then examine your inner self.'* Confucius

Throughout our lives we seek the guidance and help of other people – typically people with more years of experience than we have ourselves who can offer us insight, advice and wisdom. For many people, their grandparents have been an important source of such guidance and help. In the workplace you may have colleagues or bosses whom you feel comfortable to turn to when you are in need of some extra insight into how to deal with a problem, a situation or a person.

Advisers like these are called 'mentors', and in my working life I have been fortunate to have had a number of wise men and women who have taken me under their wings. Mentors are people to whom you can turn and trust that whatever you ask or share with them will remain confidential. They have your best interests at heart.

Today some organizations allocate at least one mentor to newly employed and/or younger members of staff. In these instances the mentor might be your boss, or even your boss's boss, but typically the mentors are senior colleagues to whom you do not report who may or may not work in the same department, team or part of the company as you do. Many organizations run support programmes, training and guidance to ensure that mentors and those whom they are mentoring have aligned expectations and understanding of mentoring's benefits and processes.

Mentoring is often linked and sometimes confused with coaching, which is the topic of the next chapter. Mentoring is essentially a process of advising, guiding and, most importantly, listening to the questions, and concerns and needs of those being mentored (sometimes called the 'mentees'); coaching is more about listening and asking questions, but not giving advice and answers.

Do not be concerned if you have never heard of mentoring or feel that you have never really benefited from a mentoring-type relationship. By following the three strategies below you can quickly come up to speed and start experiencing the benefits of having at least one mentor in your working life.

FIND A MENTOR

In looking for and selecting a mentor, many would recommend that you should start by listing the areas of knowledge, skills, understanding and guidance that you are missing and most in need of to help you succeed in your job and grow your career. Unfortunately, life is rarely this straightforward and sometimes people do not know what they need to know and understand. It is one of those lovely things about talking with a mentor – they can share insights and thoughts about which you would never have thought to enquire.

You may already have someone mentoring you well. If you have, then the advice in this chapter may not be essential for you to read in detail. But if you have a mentor and feel that you are not really receiving the kind of help and guidance that I am suggesting, please consider changing mentors – it is not worth wasting your time with someone who is not mentoring you well. Before you stop being mentored by someone, though, do explore whether you are simply not making the most of the relationship – as an example, read the strategy below and consider whether you are meeting with your mentor often enough.

If you are in need of a mentor, consider the following options:

- Is your boss a person with whom you are able to sit down and ask advice and guidance, where such advice and guidance go beyond simply asking how you do this or that? Would you feel able to trust your boss?
- Do you have conversations with any colleagues where you feel that you are already being informally mentored and guided by people who have 'been there and done that'?

You might find it useful to have more than one mentor, because different people have different experiences and knowledge. When I was a regional finance director, I had two mentors. One understood finance and accounting and our companies' reporting systems really well – he could guide me with tricky technical problems. The other was fantastic in helping to guide my career and navigate the internal politics of the UK multinational that we both worked for. Neither mentor was my boss but both were senior colleagues in related departments or regions.

MAKE TIME TO SIT DOWN WITH YOUR MENTOR(S)

We are all too busy and, without much thought, we can fill our diaries with urgent tasks and work; seemingly non-essential conversations get put off very easily. I would argue that the time you plan to spend talking with a mentor is invaluable and should be afforded the same importance as meetings with your boss, team meetings, preparing proposals, and so on. I would strongly recommend having short and regular meetings with your mentor. These could be over lunch, breakfast or coffee or simply in the office, and they might be monthly, bi-weekly or weekly, depending on how much interaction and learning you feel you want. If in doubt, meet for one hour every fortnight and see how that goes.

The key is regularity: pre-planned meetings are harder to cancel and regularity helps the mentoring to become a habit, hopefully a positive one. Attend pre-agreed mentoring sessions even if you feel that there is nothing to discuss. Why? Because mentoring is about being in the presence of someone who has a wealth of knowledge and experience and who may just ask you, 'How are things going?' or 'What have you done differently since we last met together?' Questions like this can be the start of valuable conversations. In addition, do not dismiss small talk – if there really are no mentoring topics to discuss, simply have a relaxing cup of coffee together.

APPRECIATE AND THANK YOUR MENTOR(S)

Respect the time, commitment and energy that your mentor gives as part of their role. Be on time for your meetings and try never to cancel the sessions. Remember that you need their help and support – it's not the other way round.

Also show your appreciation by following through on the things that you commit to do or to explore during the mentoring discussions. If your mentor suggests that you read a particular business book or if they pass you an article to read, then read it and never lie or pretend to have done what was asked of you. I have mentored many young people who were either entering the workforce or being promoted to more senior positions and my only moments of disappointment came when they pretended to have done something. If you cannot be honest with a mentor, I would worry that you are unable to be honest with anyone, including yourself.

Putting it all together

Throughout history people have had mentors, both in their work lives and in their personal lives. Until the last few years, mentoring support was often informal and unstructured, but organizations today are increasingly supporting mentoring programmes and, in order to ensure that you are able to achieve the levels of work success that you deserve, I urge you to have mentors throughout your working life. Don't wait to be offered a formal programme; simply follow the advice laid out in the three strategies above and benefit from your mentor's insights, knowledge and wisdom to help you work more optimally with others and achieve your goals.

Choose your mentors wisely and acknowledge your good fortune if you have already found your ideal mentors. Some people have such a good working relationship with their boss that that person is able to be an excellent mentor as well as a great coach (the subject of the next chapter). One good thing about mentors is that they are informal volunteer roles and you are not forced to stay with the same mentor for a long time: some people discover that various individuals have fulfilled mentoring roles for them over time, sometimes only being a mentor during a single conversation.

Finally, remember to make time to meet with your more formal mentors when you have pre-arranged sessions, and be grateful to anyone who gives you advice and help, no matter whether they are formally appointed mentors or simply older colleagues who are happy to share their thoughts and insights with you.

Coach and help others

'You can have everything you want in life if you just help enough people get what they want in life.' Zig Ziglar

'We make a living by what we get, we make a life by what we give.' Winston Churchill

'As you grow older you will discover that you have two hands. One for helping yourself, the other for helping others.' Audrey Hepburn

'Our prime purpose in this life is to help others and if you can't help them, at least don't hurt them.' Dalai Lama

'When you've worked hard, and done well, and walked through that doorway of opportunity, you do not slam it shut behind you. You reach back, and you give other folks the same chances that helped you succeed.' Michelle Obama

How can you really help others at work? By constantly giving others your time and attention without any expectation of a reward. This is in itself a form of success and I would encourage everyone to start acting in this way from the very first day that they enter the workforce. Quite simply, we can all give others our time and attention even when we might not be able to give knowledge or experience.

This giving of our time and attention can take many forms. Start simply having a mindset or intention of being as helpful as possible to everyone you work with. Such an intention should be a 24/7 or full-time one, not something that you switch on when you feel like doing good or because you want something in return. Some people seem to be born with what is sometimes called a 'helping gene', developed and nurtured during their younger years, and for these people helping others is as automatic as breathing. If you are not so lucky, you might have to make an extra effort to get into the habit of helping others more often.

Sometimes it is simply enough to ask someone 'Can I be of any help?' You could add whatever comments seem appropriate: 'I see that you are very busy' or 'I notice that you are new to this kind of work' or 'I realize you must be in a rush.'

Help others to explore the challenges and problems facing them through what is called 'coaching'. This is not like sports coaching, where a coach may simply tell others what to do. This is a work-based form of coaching, sometimes called executive coaching, where someone who is coaching another person asks questions which help that person to better understand and to explore the issues that concern them. Such coaching skills are becoming widely taught and used within organizations and, when they are used well, they enable people to have very open conversations with one another.

BECOME TRAINED IN COACHING SKILLS

Learning coaching skills can be an invaluable way of strengthening your people and communication skills and enabling you to be empathic. Coaching is all about helping others to improve their understanding of the issues and problems facing them and then to arrive at their own solutions and goals. I often view a coach as a mirror that asks questions. The coaching skills that you could learn either on a formal training course or simply through reading about coaching should include:

- establishing and maintaining a good level of trust with people
- seeing the positive side of other people and their potential
- listening well without jumping to conclusions or rushing to speak

- asking open-ended questions which enable others to express themselves rather than simply asking closed questions which require only a yes or no answer
- staying in the moment and focusing your attention on those with whom you are speaking
- summarizing and clarifying what others tell you, to assure them that they are being heard correctly.

Also consider becoming a certified or qualified coach. There are a number of globally recognized coaching associations and institutes which offer training courses that you could take to become qualified. I recommend the International Association of Coaching (IAC), headquartered in the USA, which also has chapters throughout the world. These can help you to become an experienced and qualified coach through the IAC Coaching Masteries. Another well-recognized coaching organization is the International Coach Federation (ICF), which has a similar model and process. With some formal training in coaching, you could offer your services to your organization as an internal coach.

EACH DAY HELP SOMEONE WHO IS NOT EXPECTING IT

One of the greatest ways of winning over other people and of being seen in a positive light is to regularly help people in both expected and unexpected ways and not to expect anything in return. For many, this is not easy – we are too used to doing and giving things in expectation of being given something back or being owed something. What I am suggesting is sometimes called unconditional helping. By giving in this way you will build up large amounts of goodwill, or what the business author Steven Covey calls building up a positive emotional bank balance.

Do not simply get into the habit of helping the same people in the same way, but rather try to do things which come as a nice surprise. I challenge you to help at least one person each day in a way that they were not expecting! These actions need not be large and could be as simple as giving your colleague a cup of coffee.

Various studies of employee engagement and surveys of employee satisfaction indicate that many people in the workplace do not feel valued. By helping your colleagues and staff in any number of ways you can contribute to increasing people's feeling of being valued, and you will also find that other people will value you more as both a colleague and a workplace friend.

HAVE COACHING CONVERSATIONS AS OFTEN AS POSSIBLE

We all spend our working days in conversations – face to face with people, on the telephone, in video conference or via emails. You may have good communication skills and feel that you are able to be part of effective conversations where you can make your points, negotiate, present, debate, etc.

I am suggesting that, when possible, you take your conversations to a different level. In conversations aim to understand first rather than simply trying to be understood; aim to listen well to other people's issues, concerns, points and arguments rather than focusing on what you want to say and present. In addition, before you rush to rebut or argue about points raised, first make sure that you are correctly hearing and understanding what others are trying to say. Sometimes this involves listening to more than just the words; it involves picking up on the feelings being expressed and reading the body language. Too many people in the workplace hide feelings and frustrations. If you can use some coaching skills, you can encourage people to share what is really troubling or concerning them and you then become someone with whom people wish to work and to whom they can turn for advice and support.

Putting it all together

By absorbing the ideas in this chapter, I am encouraging you to pause in all of your interactions with people with whom you work – not only colleagues but also customers, suppliers and anyone else you interact with in your work. By pausing, you can decide how you can be most helpful and at the same time ensure that, in all of your communications, you show that you are listening and caring and not simply giving people your views, lectures, ideas and opinions. Most people don't like being told what to do or not to do; they appreciate being helped to arrive at their own conclusions. Do you not agree?

Make a decision to start employing coaching skills in your daily interactions with your colleagues or staff and even in conversations with other stakeholders, such as clients and suppliers. You could make people's day by being so helpful.

Remember that good coaching skills require you to listen and to be non-judgemental. You are not meant to give your views and opinions, but rather to help the other person to explore their issues and problems and arrive at their own decisions and conclusions. Ideally, you can ensure that you act in this way by developing your coaching skills and even working to become a qualified coach.

12 Give others recognition and credit

❝ 'Recognition is the greatest motivator.' Gerard C. Eakedale

❝ 'There are two things people want more than sex and money… recognition and praise.' Mary Kay Ash

❝ 'People will forget what you said, people will forget what you did, but people will never forget how you made them feel.'
Maya Angelou

❝ 'I've always been an unselfish guy, and that's the only way I know how to play on the court and I try to play to the maximum of my ability – not only for myself but for my teammates.' LeBron James

❝ 'Praise can be your most valuable asset as long as you don't aim it at yourself.' Orlando A. Battista

How often do you thank your colleagues or give them some form of recognition or credit?

Successful people in the workplace like to recognize and to congratulate those around them. Too often we forget to thank and to recognize when someone else has done a great job. Ninety-nine per cent of people love and need to be valued, recognized and thanked for what they do, and studies show that praise can motivate many people more than simply giving them more money. In the workplace employees often complain that their company, their boss or their colleagues do not recognize enough the good work that they are doing. In fact, this is often cited as a reason why people resign from their jobs when they are being given exit interviews.

Not everyone openly asks for recognition – those who are more outgoing and extrovert typically actively seek recognition while those with quieter and more introverted personalities may not speak up. Some people are quite reactive and acknowledge others only when they are asked to, and a surprisingly high percentage of managers give positive praise and encouragement to their staff only once a year during the annual performance evaluation process.

Recognition and giving someone credit for something they have done or said can take many forms: it could be simply saying, 'Thank you for sharing that idea' to someone in a meeting; it could be emailing your boss to say what a great job a colleague did to help you complete a difficult project.

There is one thing worse than not giving someone thanks and recognition for something they have done and that is taking the credit for yourself. I would call this one of the most selfish acts in the workplace, but sadly it is all too common and it is the easiest way of falling out with your colleagues. A truly successful person is comfortable with themselves and with their own performance and does not need to 'steal' other people's successes to claim them as their own.

⊞ EACH DAY GIVE AT LEAST ONE PERSON THANKS AND RECOGNITION

At the end of each working day, as you travel home, ask yourself, 'To whom did I give thanks, credit or recognition today?', and answer honestly. I challenge you to develop the habit of ensuring that each day you give at least one person some form of thanks and recognition. Ideally, aim to thank and recognize a range of different people every day.

Through my years of coaching people, I have come to believe that the smallest examples of thanks and of giving others recognition in some form have a disproportionately positive effect on those being thanked and praised. I recommend that you fill your day giving thanks and credit for a multitude of small things. This behaviour will quickly become a very positive habit that will endear you to those with whom you work.

Here are some examples of small things that you could recognize:

- thanking someone for opening a door for you
- thanking the canteen staff for the great food
- having appreciative words to say to your boss's busy secretary
- recognizing people in meetings even for little things, such as drafting the agenda.

The nice thing about the giving of thanks and credit is that it is contagious – others will start copying you and you will also find that you will take the habit home.

SHARE CREDIT FOR YOUR OWN WORK

Do not take all the credit, even if you feel that the success of a task or job well done might have been down to your own efforts. It is rarely the case that all the effort was our own and often, if we think it was, we may well be deluding ourselves and thereby denying other people the thanks and credit due to them.

Try copying those Oscar-winning actors. Their acceptance speeches always seem to follow a similar script: saying that they could not have succeeded without the help and hard work of many others, thanking a long list of names of colleagues who helped them, before trying to remember to thank their spouse or parents before they are ushered off the stage!

I guess I am suggesting that you should be humble in seeking and/or accepting praise and recognition and always be ready to try to include others in the recognition process. I do recognize that different organizations have different working cultures and some organizations are more open to people seeking recognition for themselves than others. In some work environments, for example in the East, a person would never wish to be singled out for praise and recognition unless their entire group or team was also being recognized.

ENCOURAGE OTHERS (INCLUDING YOUR BOSS) TO BE MORE GENEROUS

Suggesting to someone else, particularly your own boss, that they might be a little more generous with their giving of thanks, credit and recognition can be a delicate matter and may call on your skills of diplomacy.

Often suggestions take the form of hints or reminders when the other person might be forgetting to give thanks. Such forgetfulness is often nothing more than a result of how busy we all seem to have become in today's workplaces. Recently, a banker whom I have been coaching suggested to her boss that it might be a great idea if the boss took the team out for a celebration lunch to recognize a colleague in their team who had just completed a difficult business deal. The boss had been so busy that he had totally forgotten to give public recognition to the successful member of his team.

Be proactive and speak up if you see someone lacking appropriate thanks and recognition. It is best to say something as soon as you see the need to give credit because people can be quite sensitive and may become upset if their boss or colleague forgets or is late in thanking or recognizing them.

Putting it all together

We live in a busy world where we can be asked at work to do many things, often at the same time, but there is never a good excuse for forgetting to give someone the thanks, praise or credit that they deserve for work that they have done well. Reasons to give other people recognition are numerous and can be for seemingly small things or for things that we might be taking for granted.

Successful people at work are people whom others enjoy working, connecting and communicating with. And people love to be given praise and recognition. It therefore should seem obvious that the more praise, credit and thanks you give others on a daily basis, the easier it will be for you to forge great working relationships with all those with whom you come into contact in your workplace.

So practise the three actions suggested above that will help you to develop a great habit. Give thanks and recognition on a daily basis, share credit and never, ever take someone else's credit. Encourage others, including your bosses and senior colleagues, also to give thanks and credit more often. I guarantee that your colleagues will feel more motivated and engaged and will more willingly work and connect with you if you do all of these things.

13 Network and build relationships

> 'To be successful, you have to be able to relate to people; they have to be satisfied with your personality to be able to do business with you and to build a relationship with mutual trust.' George Ross

> 'You can make more friends in two months by becoming interested in other people than you can in two years by trying to get other people interested in you.' Dale Carnegie

> 'Treasure your relationships, not your possessions.' Anthony J. D'Angelo

> 'The importance of building relationships among colleagues, of trying to create coalitions behind the issues that you are championing, was not something I ever had much insight into until I was elected and started serving in the Senate.' Hillary Clinton

> 'If you think it's hard to meet new people, try picking up the wrong golf ball.' Jack Lemmon

Working life is based on all of us connecting with other people and I am hard-pressed to think of any profession where one could avoid any human interaction. Someone is always your boss, employer, supplier, colleague, client or member of your team, and often the same person might wear more than one hat. To differing degrees you have relationships with all those with whom you work, interact or otherwise connect in your workplace. Sadly, so often people recognize someone's face and know their name but know very little else about them. This is particularly disappointing when you learn that these colleagues may have spent years both working and socializing together.

One of the main goals of the executive coaching assignments that I give is to help individuals to network more successfully in their own organizations and to be more impressive and memorable to those with whom they interact. I know of people who have been denied promotions because not enough people in their organizations knew them. A good way to test how well you have been networking and building relationships is to ask yourself how many people you could turn to for help (in terms of being introduced to other potential companies) if you were fired or laid off from your job.

Some people seem to be natural networkers and you see them at events and meetings happily talking with anyone and everyone there. Surprisingly, the people who are most successful at building genuine relationships with others are often those who seem to be quieter and less open to networking – the so-called introverts. In other words, a good networker is not necessarily the best at building and maintaining good relationships, but both are closely interlinked and merit a shared chapter in this book.

NETWORK LIKE AN EXPERIENCED EXTROVERT

Get into a mindset of understanding that meeting other people is valuable and is worth the effort. Very few people like going to functions or meetings where they are likely to know very few people. When you enter a room full of people, make an effort to go up to each person and introduce yourself and, if culturally appropriate, shake hands. Avoid the common tendency to stand and stay with the one person you recognize in the crowd of strangers. Understand that many people are nervous about meeting others and people with whom you try to 'break the ice' by introducing yourself might be relieved that you made the effort.

To help you succeed in your job and in your career, plan which people or groups of people you ought to meet, get to know and connect with. Perhaps it is some of your senior colleagues with whom you rarely connect or it might be a local Chamber of Commerce that you have been remiss in not yet joining. Be proactive; don't simply be reactive and wait for opportunities and invitations to meet with people.

Try very hard to be memorable, to have nice things to say and to be interested in the people you meet. Do you have a name card? If not, you should have some made and always try to carry them with you when you are working or even socializing. You need to enable people you have met to remember who you are, and giving them a name card is an easy way.

BE INTERESTING TO TALK WITH

Think about the new people you have met for the first time in the last few months. They might be new colleagues, clients or suppliers. What do you remember about them? Apart from perhaps remembering how they looked, you will probably recall some of the conversations that you had and I would guess that you will more easily remember those people with whom you had interesting and memorable conversations.

No matter how uncomfortable you feel, try to have conversations that are always equally interesting and memorable. Start by making small talk and, no matter what you ask or say, sound genuine and interested. Secondly, have a few funny stories or jokes to hand, but only use them if it is appropriate to lighten the mood and always be culturally sensitive. Thirdly, be ready to ask questions rather than to talk about yourself – people love to talk about themselves, so let the people you meet do that. You could adopt the coaching conversation model from Secret 11 – having a conversation where you listen well and allow the other person or group of people to speak more. It is also important that others learn who you are, so be ready to talk about yourself but ideally wait until after the other person has shared first. Finally, be natural and look for areas of genuine mutual interest that could be the basis for ongoing interaction between you.

NURTURE IMPORTANT AND LONG-TERM WORK RELATIONSHIPS

Try to avoid the mistake of losing touch with people with whom you used to have a connection. List the most important people in your working life – include those who have helped you to get to where you are today and are helping you to grow and hopefully be promoted. They might be current or former bosses, mentors, colleagues or people who report to you. For each of the people on your list, think through how well you are connecting and keeping in touch with each of them. If you have been moving cities or even countries during your career, have you made an effort to keep in touch with those important past colleagues?

I strongly recommend that you make an extra effort to keep in contact with them all. Perhaps you find them on social media and connect online (for example, through LinkedIn or Facebook) or invite them for lunch or a drink. Successful people like to keep in touch with people with whom they have connected and they are normally generous and willing to help and support them as needed.

Unless you work in a cave as a solitary hermit, your entire working life will involve connecting with people. Some may be quite junior and low paid while others might be in senior positions with global job roles. This chapter reminds you never to hold back from meeting and connecting with new people and people you already know. Do not wait until you have a particular issue or problem before reconnecting with someone. If you do, then your connections might feel that you are just taking advantage of them. Connect with people in moments when you have no pressing shared work issues and you can instead talk about yourselves and get to know each other. An Australian hospice nurse recently reported that, on their deathbeds, people often regret working too hard and not connecting with and spending enough time with people who mattered to them.

For most people, particularly introverts, more networking and building of relationships can be uncomfortable and it may involve having to step outside your comfort zone. I challenge you to let this happen and I can assure you that you will be pleasantly surprised by the range of new people you will meet and the depth of friendships that will develop.

14 Align with your employer's mission and vision

❝ 'The most empowering condition of all is when the entire organization is aligned with its mission, and people's passions and purpose are in synch with each other.' Bill George Peter Sims

❝ 'When you have vision it affects your attitude. Your attitude is optimistic rather than pessimistic.' Charles R. Swindoll

❝ 'If you want to build a ship, don't herd people together to collect wood and don't assign them tasks and work, but rather teach them to long for the endless immensity of the sea.'
Antoine de Saint-Exupéry

❝ 'Effectiveness without values is a tool without a purpose.'
Edward de Bono

❝ 'Efforts and courage are not enough without purpose and direction.' John F. Kennedy

Does your employer have a mission or a vision statement and, if they have, have you ever read them?

A mission statement describes what we do as an organization and what makes us different from similar organizations. It typically defines the purpose and goals of the organization, setting out how the organization will get where it wants to be.

A vision statement is very similar and explains where the organization aims to be and normally reflects a combination of the purpose and values of the organization.

61

You may have seen these statements on the walls of your own employer or when visiting other organizations. Think of a well-known company and you can Google their mission and vision statements. Some organizations only have one statement, which is normally called 'the mission'. Here are examples of mission statements taken from two well-known company's websites:

'Facebook's mission is to give people the power to share and make the world more open and connected.'

'The BMW Group is the world's leading provider of premium products and premium services for individual mobility.'

The most successful people in the workplace are those who normally really like and 'buy into' their employer's mission and vision – in other words, people who like what the company wishes to achieve and where it is heading. It is akin to being on a ship and liking what the ship is doing and where the vessel is heading. Can you imagine being on a ship and not wishing to go where it is heading?

In an ideal world you should be working in an organization where you are in total agreement and alignment with your employer's purpose and direction. If you feel that there is a misalignment, then you have three options:

- try to accept that there is a difference (in other words, change your own attitude)
- try to change the organization's purpose and direction
- find a new organization to work for.

KNOW YOUR OWN PURPOSE AND DIRECTION

Before you concern yourself with your employer's mission and vision, it is essential that you know yourself better and answer the following questions:

- What do I wish to be and to become?
- What is my purpose?
- How do I wish to get there?

This links to the discussion in Secret 1, where you were encouraged to explore your dreams and passions.

Then reflect on and answer the following question honestly: are you best able to achieve these aims in your current job and with your existing employer? This connects with the next strategy below.

DETERMINE IF YOU ARE COMFORTABLE WITH YOUR EMPLOYER'S PURPOSE AND DIRECTION

I often ask participants in my leadership workshops whether any of them know their employer's mission or vision. Very few of them have any idea. I then ask them, 'Why therefore are you working for your employer? Would you take a plane journey if you had no idea where it was heading or how it operated?' In fact, too many people work in organizations where they have no real idea about their employer's purpose and direction.

I challenge you to go and find out whether your employer has a mission or a vision. Speak with a senior leader to double-check whether the wording of the statement(s) is the most up-to-date version and that this truly reflects where the organization is heading and what it is aiming to achieve. I then encourage you to ask yourself what you feel about what the statements are saying. Do you like what they stand for and do you feel motivated to help your employer to achieve their aims?

As an example, what do you feel about the Facebook and BMW mission statements above? Do they excite you and make you feel that you would like working for those companies?

Think through how you can become more aligned to, motivated by and excited by your own employer's mission and vision. Often it is simply a matter of better understanding, which normally involves hearing from senior leaders themselves what the mission and vision really mean.

There are extreme cases where people feel that they really cannot adapt to accept, flow with and work with an organization's purpose and direction. This could be for any number of reasons, which may include the aims seeming too boring, too challenging, unambitious, unethical or even illegal. If you felt like that, it is highly unlikely that you would be motivated to succeed in the organization. I know of a friend who turned down a major promotion at a fizzy drinks company because he realized that he could no longer spend his time helping to grow a company which simply sold drinks filled with sugar.

If you have tried but really feel that you are not comfortable with your employer's purpose and direction, it is probably better to move on and find an organization where you can be more aligned. This can also enable you to motivate yourself better and be more successful. Life is too short to stay in the wrong place.

ENCOURAGE YOUR COLLEAGUES TO BE ALIGNED

Assuming that you are comfortable with and supportive of your employer's purpose and direction, be ready to help those with whom you work to become comfortable too. There may be times when your colleagues say things such as:

- I have no idea where our company is heading and I think we have lost direction as a company.
- We seem to be wasting money on all of these new product developments and changing direction without any logic.

When you hear comments like these, you could practise your newly acquired coaching skills and engage your colleague in a productive and positive discussion to help remind him or her that the glass is half full and not half empty. Playing this role is akin to being an ambassador for your company, and this is discussed more in a later chapter.

Putting it all together

If this is the first time that you have ever thought about your employer's mission or vision statements, I do hope that you liked what you found and do not feel that you are on the wrong ship heading to a destination that you have no interest in visiting!

Remember that you must know where you want to head yourself and what your own purpose is. You then need to know your employer's purpose and direction and ask yourself whether you are in the right place – are you aligned and wanting to head where your employer is taking you? This is not a scientific process and you may not be totally sure but, as a minimum, following the three strategies in this chapter will enable you to be more self-aware and will have helped you to understand your employer better.

Hopefully, you now know your employer's mission and/or vision statements and are quite comfortable with the organization's purpose and the direction it is taking. If you do not feel aligned to your organization's purpose and direction, talk about this with people you trust. Talk with your boss and some of your senior colleagues: when you learn more, you may become more comfortable and accepting. If you are not able to accept where the company is heading, be open to the idea of moving on to find an organization where you can feel more comfortable and be more successful.

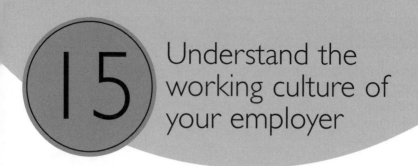

15 Understand the working culture of your employer

There are many definitions of a culture and my definition would be that an organization's culture is the combination of how the people in that organization work and interact together. A culture can be visible in people's values and in how people communicate, behave, think, make decisions and generally operate throughout the working day, and a culture comes out in what people expect of others and the norms that people consciously or unconsciously follow. You may have heard people making comments such as 'He is a company man' or 'He is not one of us' or 'You can see that she has not adapted to our working culture.'

A particular working culture can be observed in numerous ways in a workplace, including these examples:

- Some working cultures value people who speak up and challenge; others do not.
- Some working cultures value timeliness – meetings always start on time and latecomers are viewed negatively – whereas in other organizations it is normal and acceptable to be late and people often have to be given reminders.

Sometimes the differences between organizations' working cultures can be seen in very small and unusual ways. I know of one company where people never open the door for anyone else and I was criticized for doing so. I was also recently made fun of for turning up to a technology company's office for a meeting wearing a shirt and tie, with someone asking me why I was being so formal.

When one company is acquired by or merges with another company, one of the biggest challenges is how to persuade people to adapt to and accept a new working culture. A global organization's working culture is also influenced and affected by the distinctive cultures of different countries, regions and ethnic groups. Successful people understand their employer's ethos well and will have learned to adapt to and accept its cultural expectations and norms.

UNDERSTAND YOUR WORKING CULTURE'S NORMS AND EXPECTATIONS

Many people join new companies and do not last very long – either resigning or being asked to leave. One of the main reasons is because they failed to adapt to the organization's working culture. In truth, it is normally not a 'failure to adapt' but rather a failure to understand the new company's working culture and its norms and expectations.

Even if you have been working for many years in your company, you may not be able to explain what your employer's working culture is. This is often because you are so used to the way things are and you have nothing to compare your own employer's working culture to. I can assure you, though, that you would immediately start observing how different everything seemed if you were to move to a completely new company.

I would like to suggest that you learn to understand well your employer's working culture in the following ways:

- Watch how people operate, act and interact. What patterns do you observe? Where you see many people doing things in similar ways, it is probable that those behaviours or habits could be viewed as elements of your organization's working culture.
- After any new colleagues have worked in your company for at least a couple of weeks, sit down with them over a coffee and explore what differences they have observed and experienced between where they used to work and your current workplace.

ADAPT TO AND ACCEPT THE WORKING CULTURE

Once you understand the working culture of your workplace, you then need to resolve to work optimally within the culture. As mentioned earlier, many successful people appear to be able to do this effortlessly and they flow with how their colleagues and bosses act and operate.

The key is not to appear out of place in your workplace and, if you do, then at least be aware of it. Examples of how you may need to adapt are numerous and might include things such as:

- understanding the dress code and when it is a norm to dress down or casually
- when emailing people, there will be accepted norms of how long emails should be and/or who it is appropriate to copy in
- in meetings there might be a pattern of how topics are discussed, how much debate takes place or how long presentations generally are.

I am not suggesting that you should robotically copy everyone else in how they work, but I do urge you to be fully aware of and, to a degree, manage how well you appear to fit in and flow with how others operate.

This is a particularly important strategy to follow when you are moving to a new department, team or organization. It is also applicable when you are given a new boss to report to because you need to align yourself with his or her working culture.

HELP NEW PEOPLE JOINING YOUR ORGANIZATION

When a new person joins your company and you come into contact with them – perhaps they are a colleague, part of your team or simply someone you meet in the canteen – I would encourage you to give them some of your knowledge and advice about the company.

Your human resources department colleagues might help new members of staff to join and to settle into your organization, but it is unlikely that they will share details about the working culture with them. You would be doing your new colleagues a big favour if you were to tell them about the ways things are done in your workplace – email etiquette, how meetings are run, how long particular presentations typically last, etc. I would suggest that you might share all those things which you wish you had known when you first joined the organization.

Putting it all together

The working culture in an organization is rarely spoken about and is often only discussed when someone is critical about where they are working. This is a shame because the working culture influences and affects everything around you. It is important to try to understand not only the working culture in which you work but also how well you are fitting into its norms and expectations.

It is okay to be different from your colleagues in some respects – different in how you address people, or different in how you write emails, or different in how you chair meetings – but much of the time it is wise to flow with the culture. As an example, if people in your company always 'cc' their bosses in certain types of emails, then I would recommend that you do the same unless you genuinely believe that it is better for you to act differently. It will be hard to be successful in your role if you act differently from other people and you are viewed negatively as a result, perhaps being seen as odd and not wishing to 'play along'.

Once you have come to understand the different aspects of your organization's working culture, you can then decide how you align your behaviour with how other people operate. Finally, in order to make friends with new colleagues, consider how you might helpfully share with them insights into different aspects of the working culture in your organization.

Understand and work with office politics

> 'Politics is the food of sense exposed to the hunger of folly.'
> Fulke Greville

> 'Man is by nature a political animal.' Aristotle

> 'Many promising executives derail sometime during their careers, often because they weren't very good at office politics.' Prof. Jeffrey Pfeffer

> 'I realized that talent would get me as far as middle management, but beyond that point it would become a matter of politics and currying favour with bosses.' Masahiro Origuchi

> 'I never repeat gossip, so listen carefully.' Anonymous

Many successful people fail in their careers because they never quite understand or deal well with what's going on around them. These people might be technically very strong but may lack the ability or desire to play along with the different aspects of what we crudely call 'office politics'.

Office politics in an organization are in some ways an aspect of the working culture's norms and expectations and can best be described as a combination of:

- the informal and often social groups of colleagues within a department or organization
- the degree to which people are close, loyal and supportive of certain individuals or groups

- how people may be negative in some way about other colleagues and how they communicate this
- the existence of informal leaders and spokespersons for vested interests and interest groups
- the ways in which groups of people need to be won over or make allies
- the ways in which news, gossip and messages are spread and shared.

I would say that calling all of this office politics is very apt because someone who is able to successfully navigate through or work with these things has to be very political – political in the work friends they make, political about who they have lunch with, political in who they share ideas with to get feedback or to let others know something.

Office politics are not easily described. I think it best simply to say that, to ensure that you are successful in your work and career, you really need to be ready to understand the different ways in which people act and communicate together, in much the same way as you have to understand the broader working culture. You must also decide whether you are comfortable with the type and level of office politics in your current organization. I have known many people who felt that they could not operate well within the office politics and chose to resign. I hope that this never happens to you but, if that is the only way in which you could ensure success in your career, then you must make such brave decisions.

OBSERVE THE OFFICE POLITICS OCCURRING AROUND YOU

Step back and observe the range of office politics that you see around you at work. You might wish to draw a diagram of the different groupings among your colleagues, asking yourself such questions as who seems to be supporting the promotion of your boss or who is speaking negatively about a planned merger. I encourage you simply to be aware and conscious of your part in all of this, asking yourself, 'Why might I be seen to be taking sides or trying to be close to certain people?'

Having gained a perspective on the office politics around you, explore those parts that seem material or important to you and decide what part you will play. Might you choose to join those opposing or supporting something? Might you actively try to befriend a certain colleague who may have undue influence over something?

MAKE THE RIGHT FRIENDS AT WORK

You may be fortunate to work in a very small organization where you have had the time to get to know well and become friends with all of your new colleagues. If, however, you are not so fortunate, you may need to be a little more selective about who you make an effort to connect with. Our time is normally limited and it may not be possible to befriend and spend enough time with everyone who seems to matter.

In an ideal world you could simply connect only with those colleagues with whom you actually come into contact during the working day and for many people this is precisely what they do. But this is not enough if you truly wish to succeed in your work and you may need to befriend other key people, but not in a way that makes it obvious that you are only being friendly for political reasons. It is always useful to get to know those colleagues who are being very successful and are often spoken about as being groomed or prepared for bigger roles in your organization. As these people are promoted and rise, you would hope that they would take you up with them, in the sense of them being supportive of your role and contribution.

I was recently coaching someone working in a bank who had missed out on a promotion that she really hoped to be offered. The reason? That she was not known by some of the key decision-makers, with one of them simply saying, 'Who is she?'

DO NOT SELL YOUR SOUL

Beware of playing along with any office politics so well that you end up, for example, becoming engrossed by gossiping and spreading negative stories which potentially affect someone's work, character or how they are perceived.

You might choose to make friends with particular colleagues just to win favour and to be liked by certain people. If you feel compelled to do this, do it with your eyes wide open. Try not to pretend to like people if you do not and do not always agree with what such people think, do and say just to avoid upsetting or falling out with them.

Always try to be fair and balanced and avoid doing the things which you know to be wrong, such as 'stabbing someone in the back', in order to be liked or be popular with certain groups of colleagues. I have done this before by allowing myself to gossip about a colleague and, although I may have benefited in the short term by being seen to be playing along with views of a certain group of supposedly influential colleagues, I regretted what I did. The person who I spoke badly of never spoke to me again after hearing about the gossip, in spite of me apologizing. It is very easy to get carried away when in a group and it takes great strength to disagree, speak up or walk away when people are playing politics and are 'throwing mud' at particular colleagues by making unnecessary and negative comments.

Putting it all together

Mastering and navigating around office politics is never easy and there are times when you may simply be on the receiving end of some negative gossip or rumours. Put any group of people together and the signs of office politics always seem to emerge as different groupings form, with gossiping, people opposing others and all of this typically happening in very informal ways that you may not be aware of unless you are particularly observant. So often I have given career coaching to individuals who had no idea that they were to be fired or laid off until the moment it had happened. However, afterwards they discovered that other people knew that their laying off was going to happen or was at least on the cards.

In some organizations the office-politics-related conversations and gossip can be the main source of information for many of the staff about what is really happening, with details of who is on the way up or on the way down often being shared.

You are therefore urged to become an expert in your organization's office politics and related gossip and advised to work consciously to be known by and to befriend those leaders and colleagues who seem to be the ones of most influence and/or rising in your organization.

Finally, take heed of my earlier advice about not 'selling out' or 'selling your soul' – do not seek the favour of some by speaking badly of others. Equally, if someone is seemingly not succeeding and may even be at risk of being laid off and you have been close to them, do not suddenly desert them or start staying away from them. Show understanding and compassion and perhaps warn your colleague of what you are hearing and, if you feel compelled, speak up in support of them.

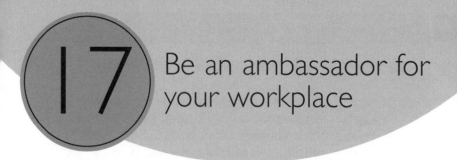

17 Be an ambassador for your workplace

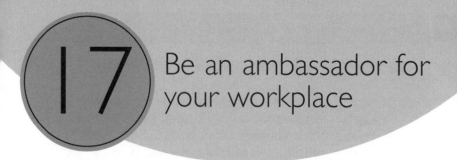 'Speak ill of no man, but speak all the good you know of everybody.' Benjamin Franklin

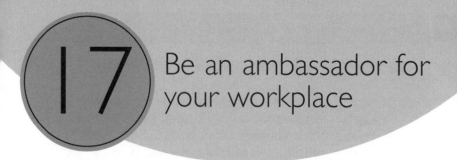 'Before you speak ask yourself if what you are going to say is true, is kind, is necessary, is helpful. If the answer is no, maybe what you are about to say should be left unsaid.' Bernard Meltzer

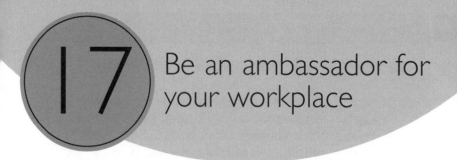 'Life is a shipwreck but we must not forget to sing in the lifeboats.' Voltaire

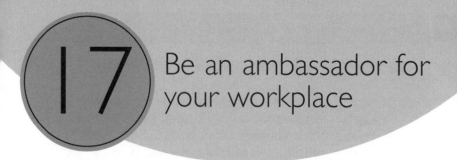 'A person who has good thoughts cannot ever be ugly... but if you have good thoughts they will shine out of your face like sunbeams and you will always look lovely.' Roald Dahl

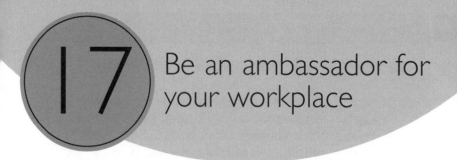 'We are all in the gutter, but some of us are looking at the stars.' Oscar Wilde

When I entered the workforce, a family friend gave me some sound advice which I have always tried to follow: 'Never speak badly of where you work or of those with whom you work; and, if you feel tempted to, stay silent.' If only we could all only speak well of our bosses and the organizations in which we work. It is so common to listen to people who are complaining bitterly about their company – saying they make terrible products, managers are lazy, they hire poor-quality graduates, they lie to customers, etc.

In my global travels I have had the pleasure of getting to know some of those lifelong career diplomats who represent their countries. These individuals never say anything that could be construed in any way as negative about their own countries and governments. They are extremely diplomatic and only express what is good and positive. To truly succeed in any workplace we must emulate diplomats.

To be admired by your bosses and colleagues, it is not enough simply to stay silent when you might otherwise wish to say something negative. Instead, I would encourage you to actively speak highly of what your bosses and colleagues are doing. Some people are so naturally positive that they only feel comfortable and enjoy seeing the positive in people and situations around them.

In addition, you should also speak highly of your past employers as well as of your current employer. Although you might have left a company, it might make your current colleagues and bosses feel uncomfortable about you if you speak ill of your past employers and may make you sound ungrateful. Colleagues may also wonder what negative things you might choose to say about your current employer.

WATCH WHAT YOU ARE SAYING (VERBALLY AND NON-VERBALLY)

It is surprising how blind we can be to what we are communicating both verbally and non-verbally. 'I never spoke badly about our company.' This is what an ex-colleague said after he was laid off partly because of what his boss cited as his lack of support, and indeed active non-support, of the company's growth plans and strategy. In the case of my friend, I think that he was seen to fail not so much by speaking against the company's plans but by not speaking in favour – both internally and when connecting with external stakeholders.

If you find it hard to observe yourself well, why not ask some of your team or colleagues to warn you if you ever start speaking negatively about your bosses or the organization in which you work. I know of someone who put some money into a collection tin for a charity every time he caught himself saying something negative. Similarly, you could also ask those same people to point out when you say something positive.

MAKE AN EXTRA EFFORT TO SAY POSITIVE THINGS IN PUBLIC

A country's experienced ambassadors are trained to speak highly of their government's policies and actions at all times, even when they may not personally agree with what is happening. If you wish to be viewed positively by those with whom you work, try always to observe and talk about the good in things that your company, department, boss or team is doing.

There is, of course, a place to speak up with criticism and potentially non-supportive thoughts – typically in meetings and discussions where ideas and plans are being considered. But, once a decision has been made to head in a particular direction, you should act positively and supportively. The decisions might involve many things, both small and large, for instance who is promoted or hired into a certain role, where the next Christmas party will be held, who is chosen to represent the company at a conference, the choice of company chosen to merge with in a certain country. The list of things which you can choose either to support as an ambassador or to speak negatively about is endless.

Learn to pause before you say anything that is not positive. If something about what your boss or company is doing is upsetting you, reflect and pause before you rush to gossip negatively and complain. I have known so many colleagues over the years who said a bit too much and were either told off by their boss or, worse, given a warning letter or fired. I urge and encourage people to share their feelings in private with their boss and other relevant colleagues but in public to 'tow the line' and show support. In many cultures, such as in Asia and in the Middle East, it is of the utmost importance to be seen to be supportive to avoid any risk of leaders appearing to lack the support of their teams – often called 'losing face'.

I will add that you can 'fake it until you can make it' – you can learn to act and sound positive and supportive even when you may be feeling quite the opposite inside. If you do this often enough, you might actually find that you will be less resistant and will feel less negative about things happening in your organization than you used to.

ENCOURAGE OTHERS TO COPY YOUR POSITIVE LEAD

Encouraging others not to moan, be negative or be unduly critical of something takes a certain amount of courage and tact. I have developed the skill of acting this way and I know that it can make me unpopular at times but I persist. I try to use tact, saying things such as, 'Come on, guys, let's try to see the positive side of the company's decision' or 'I know that we are upset that our colleague was not promoted into the key role, but let's not waste our time moaning and gossiping about it.'

Putting it all together

Coming to work each day and speaking highly and positively of everything would take extreme effort and is probably not possible. We all experience and hear things that upset us or that we do not agree with. I have no doubt that, inside the walls of their embassy, ambassadors often get into difficult discussions and debates and sometimes also push against suggestions from the home country's foreign ministry. But, in public, the ambassador puts on a smile and supports whatever initiative or idea has been agreed by their government.

Act like an ambassador: there is no need for you to wear a hat on your head or a lapel badge stating that you are now an ambassador, but have that mindset. In summary, this will involve a combination of watching what you say, holding back in public when you have nothing positive or helpful to say, making an extra effort to be more supportive of what your company and bosses are doing, and encouraging your colleagues to follow your lead. You will be surprised at how the working culture and office politics can all start to become more positive. You may even find that you will all start being less critical of what your partners and children are doing when you and your colleagues go home!

18 Accept and embrace change

Everything is constantly changing – we all get a little older and more experienced in work and our organizations are constantly facing new and varied challenges with clients, suppliers, staff and a myriad of other stakeholders. We try to create budgets and forecasts of what will happen in our businesses but so often the reality will be different. In working life nothing seems to stay the same and business-school thinking seems to accelerate this by promoting the need for organizations to keep evolving and changing.

Humans do not seem to like change and the majority of people with whom I have worked actually hate leaving the status quo of their comfort zones. New bosses, new systems, new products and new client requests can often be greeted with resistance, and this can have any number of negative effects on a business, from friction and stress through to delays and upset clients.

Changes can be of any size and people will still react in the same way – being either against the change or more open to accepting the change. One of my past colleagues used to become angry when our company canteen changed the menu without giving warning. Not surprisingly, he would sometimes erupt in terrible anger when larger changes were affecting him at work.

People who are truly successful at work have learned to accept and to embrace change and to go with the flow of changes in their work environment. They seem to understand that change is inevitable and they do not wish to be left behind. In fact, they are often the first to support and to productively help implement needed changes in their workplace.

So much of how we deal with change relates to our mindset and how we choose to react in the face of new or different information. You can always spot those colleagues who have been through a lot of varied changes in their careers – aside from them potentially having grey hairs, they seem to react more calmly, be more reflective and listen well when changes are happening to them or around them.

The following strategies will enable you to act in these more mature ways to whatever kinds of change come to you in your work.

UNDERSTAND THE STAGES OF DEALING WITH CHANGE

There seems be a predictable process that people pass through when facing and having to deal with any kind of change in the workplace. This process has been compared to the stages of grieving when a loved one has died. The process typically starts with being in denial, then being upset and angry before resisting and then finally accepting. Be ready to understand that you and those you work with might react to change by being seemingly stuck in any of these four stages:

1. **Disregard and denial** – Some people appear to 'put their head in the sand' and try to act as if there is no change being proposed or actually happening. This can become a bad habit for some people.

2. **Anger and upset** – Have you ever been upset when something around you is being changed? Some people can be quite emotional and hold on to such upset and anger. This can really affect their ability to be objective and balanced.
3. **Fighting and resistance** – Some people openly oppose changes while others might appear to be publicly supporting them but still be resisting, for example by being very slow in helping to implement their part of any change.
4. **Adapting and acceptance** – This is the ideal stage, which one hopes everybody can arrive at as soon as possible and avoid getting stuck in any of the earlier three stages.

Do you ever become stuck in any of the first three stages? Awareness can be the starting point for working through ways in which you react to change in any negative way that could be construed as being resistant to or against that particular change.

WORK ON YOUR OWN AREAS OF WEAKNESS

Here are some words of advice about how you can avoid getting stuck in any of the first three stages of the process of dealing with change outlined above. Be honest with yourself about how you react to change – I do not know of anyone who, when faced with changes, can honestly say that they never acted in denial, got angry and upset or fought and resisted. All humans exhibit at least one of these three stages, even if it is for only a short time.

If you find yourself choosing to ignore and deny changes that are being imposed on or asked of you, it is good to ask yourself why. Perhaps you have a habit of delaying difficult conversations and dealing with change falls into the same category? Perhaps you have grown to dislike bad news and you view change as a bad thing? Overcoming one's denial of change is about altering your mindset and, in my experience, you might need the help of your colleagues. I would recommend that you ask a couple of them to tell you as soon as they sense that you are ignoring a change that you have been asked to make or that needs to happen around you.

What do you do if you are someone who has a pattern of getting upset and/or angry in the face of change? In extreme cases you might benefit from seeking anger management help or seeing a therapist. Thankfully, in the vast majority of cases, nothing so drastic is required and you need only to become more mindful and to pause before you react to any kind of change-related issues. Here again, you could seek the support of a few trusted colleagues or even your boss and ask them to tell you to stop as soon as they sense that you might be emotionally overreacting to something.

Finally, how might you stop fighting and resisting any changes, if this is one of your habits? This can be a self-destructive and addictive attitude and I know of many otherwise great employees who have been fired for opposing and fighting changes that their boss or organization wished to implement. At the risk of oversimplifying this topic, I would say this: *learn to accept what you cannot change and not to oppose that which you do not wish to accept.*

LEAD OTHERS THROUGH THE CHANGE PROCESS

No matter whether you are a formal leader or simply a member of a team, you can choose to help those colleagues who may not be dealing with change very well. They could be facing any number of possible changes – it might be a new database system that your department must adopt, or perhaps a new boss being appointed who comes with a very different working culture.

Simply help walk your colleagues through the first two strategies listed above. That is all you can do – you are leading them to water but they must choose to drink it!

Putting it all together

Surveys and anecdotal evidence consistently show that people and entire organizations have trouble dealing with and implementing all kinds of changes. Too many of us in the workplace act too complacently and prefer not to have to change.

To truly excel at work, you must learn to be comfortable exploring new ideas and suggestions which may, in turn, lead to changes needing to be implemented. In doing so, you can become what is called a change agent, who is able to help all of those around to overcome the three stages that can cause changes to fail to be implemented successfully, namely denial, anger and resistance.

I recognize that getting people to the point of understanding and acceptance of the need to change is never easy. Sometimes the smallest changes can cause an organization the most angst and one might argue that change is constantly occurring and it is simply a question of whether we are flowing with it or opposing it. If you can be seen by your bosses as someone who readily embraces change and attempts to see the positive in any changes, then you are increasing your value. Your mindset and attitude will be invaluable in helping the organization to grow and move forward through whatever kinds of changes are deemed necessary.

19) Always do the right thing

❝ *'Do the right thing. It will gratify some people and astonish the rest.'* Mark Twain

❝ *'Have the courage to say no. Have the courage to face the truth. Do the right thing because it is right. These are the magic keys to living your life with integrity.'* W. Clement Stone

❝ *'Keep a good attitude and do the right thing even when it's hard.'* Joel Olsteen

❝ *'All the mistakes I ever made were when I wanted to say "no" and said "yes".'* Moss Hart

❝ *'Learn to say "no" to the good so you can say "yes" to the best.'* John C. Maxwell

There may be times when you are asked, expected or encouraged to do or say something at work which you feel is incorrect, inappropriate or downright wrong. I am sure that you have experienced this and here are some of the kinds of examples that are quite common:

- You are asked to lie on behalf of your boss, for example confirming that he was with you in a meeting when in truth he was not.
- You are asked to alter some forecast or budget numbers to show your department in a better light, for example numbers that are more easily beaten.

- You are expected to lie to a customer about a delivery date commitment when your team knows that the products will be late.
- You are asked to pretend to a supplier that future orders will be large in order to negotiate a lower purchase price today for a particular raw material or service, when you know that the future volumes will be low.
- You know that your colleague is paying a bribe to a client to help win an order.
- You observe colleagues being sexist or in other ways discriminatory and you are expected to play along because you are being told that behaviour of this kind is in some sense acceptable.

This chapter is closely aligned to Chapter 5's discussion of truth and integrity and it is key that you reflect and explore when it is right to play along and say 'yes' or to take a stand and say 'no'. You will probably face the dilemma in situations where you feel that you should say 'no' but that this will affect your relationships with your boss and/or colleagues and may even negatively impact upon your career prospects.

With larger issues, when you make a decision to say 'no', you may become what is referred to as a whistle-blower who exposes activity which is in some way illegal. Many organizations have written codes of conduct and related policies and you would be expected to do the right thing. The challenge comes from having colleagues and bosses who may have another opinion when it comes to a particular issue, behaviour or topic.

PRACTISE SAYING 'NO' WHEN YOU NORMALLY SAID 'YES'

This 'do I or don't I' dilemma challenges you in terms of your character, ethics, integrity and morals. The easiest answer, which often is the best for your career, at least in the short term, is to accept what is happening around you and avoid being seen as a 'tell-tale' or whistle-blower.

Only you can decide when you are willing and ready to stand firm and do the right thing, in terms of what is ethically and legally correct, even if this risks damaging your career at your current employer. This is one of the most delicate and tricky topics contained in this entire book. If it is any consolation, some of today's great business leaders such as Sir Richard Branson, Jack Welch and Steve Jobs would say: 'Always do what you know is the right thing to do, every time without question.'

Practise doing what you feel is right, remembering the words of an old Sting song: 'Be yourself no matter what they say.' It might start when you tell a colleague that how they are treating a female colleague is wrong; it might be in refusing to change some numbers in a spreadsheet.

If you need to seek advice and support, find yourself a mentor in your company whom you trust and with whom you can share your predicament. If you are not comfortable speaking with a senior colleague, find someone else – perhaps an experienced relative or another colleague with plenty of work experience.

BE HONEST WITH YOURSELF, EVEN IF YOU SAY 'YES'

I know that this advice to always say 'no' when you may be pressured to say 'yes' may sound easy but I also know that it is one of the hardest things to do when you are at work. Colleagues may ostracize you and call you disloyal.

You may retort that you have a house loan and other financial commitments and so you cannot risk losing your job by 'rocking the boat', and therefore there may be times when you feel you have to say 'yes' even when in your heart you know you ought to have said 'no'. If you really must play along when you know you should not, then at least do so with your eyes open. Be totally honest with yourself about what you are doing. Know that it is wrong and do not fool yourself by thinking that your actions are somehow okay – it is not okay to turn a blind eye to sexual harassment, it is not okay to lie to clients or suppliers, it is not okay to cheat on expenses. You know when it is not okay.

BE READY TO LOOK FOR A NEW JOB

If by 'doing the right' thing you might jeopardize your career prospects with your employer, then I would say that you need to seriously consider finding a new employer with better values and a better working culture. You cannot hope to be a person of integrity and to be successful in a workplace where you are being put under pressure to be deceitful or to cheat or lie.

Excelling at work is only possible if you feel you are in the ideal environment where you are able to truly express yourself and to act with your desired level of integrity and ethics.

If you feel trapped by house loan mortgage payments or other financial commitments and you dare not risk losing your job, you might consider seeking the help of an executive coach or a career coach. The aim of the coaching would be to try to make you as comfortable as possible with your choices and with working in an organization that you might prefer to leave.

Putting it all together

The topic of this chapter is rarely written about but I feel strongly that it is an area which must be explored by anyone wishing to truly excel in their work. You might have been lucky in your career to date and you may not have faced any moments where you had to ask yourself whether you speak up or go along with something that is not ideal. But you never know what might happen in the future and there may come a time when one of your colleagues could be facing the 'doing the right thing' dilemma and may turn to you for advice. In such an event this chapter will be of use.

Trying to do what is right will often entail you having to disagree with others, and this is not easy. Once you start doing it more often, you will find it easier, partly because your colleagues will begin to expect it and may even begrudgingly respect you for saying and doing what you believe is right.

Even if you find you cannot always say 'no' to something when you are being pushed to say 'yes', you are strongly encouraged to be honest with yourself and never to start kidding yourself that it is okay to do the wrong thing. It is always really helpful to seek the guidance and support of trusted senior colleagues or friends. Always remember that you may reach a point when your conscience will be compelling you to act, and it might then be time to resign and move on. You can find a new workplace in which to excel!

20 Work beyond your job description

> 'Always do more than is required of you.' General George Patton

> 'Do more than is required. What is the distance between someone who achieves their goals consistently and those who spend their lives and careers merely following? The extra mile.' Gary Ryan Blair

> 'There are no traffic jams along the extra mile.' Roger Staubach

> 'Today, and every day, deliver more than you are getting paid to do. Make yourself so valuable in your work that eventually you will become indispensable.' Og Mandino

> 'You can start right where you stand and apply the habit of going the extra mile by rendering more service and better service than you are now being paid for.' Napoleon Hill

Every successful person I have ever known has always been willing to do more than they are asked to do and also paid to do. How willing are you to emulate such people by 'going the extra mile' and always doing more than is expected of you?

Today, in your job, do you know exactly what is expected of you in terms of your actual role and responsibilities? Perhaps, when you started in your current job role, you were shown a job description or perhaps you were asked to help draft one. I know of many former colleagues and people I have coached who have complained either that they had never seen a job description or that what they had seen bore no relevance to what they actually had to do. It is obviously hard to do more than is expected of you if you do not actually know what that is. But in truth what is expected of you relates to what your boss and other relevant colleagues expect of you and they will most probably not compare your productivity and performance with what is written in a job description. Instead they will compare how you perform with their own expectations, how other people in comparable roles perform and how any predecessor in your role performed.

Being noticed and hopefully acknowledged by your bosses and peers for doing things which are beyond what you are expected to do is normally a very good thing and could help you to be promoted. There is an old saying that, if you wish to be promoted, start doing your new job now – in other words, make time to do work that relates to the tasks involved in the role that you hope to be promoted into. Some people might call you a workaholic who is simply trying to please the boss, and to some extent such a comment would have truth to it. The three strategies below will walk you through how to do this extra work without letting it burn you out or seem too obvious a case of trying to please your boss.

KNOW WHAT IS EXPECTED OF YOU AND CONSCIOUSLY DO MORE

Before you think about taking on extra tasks and 'going the extra mile', make sure that you know what is expected of you in your current role by your bosses and that you are fulfilling these expectations. You do not wish to be taking on extra work while being seen to be neglecting your normal and expected work.

Once you know what you should be doing and are completing those tasks well, you are then in a position to then take on more and to 'go the extra mile'.

BECOME INVALUABLE WITHOUT BURNING OUT

Virtually no one can claim to be in a job role where it would be so difficult to replace them that they are indispensable. I have never met such a person, but I have met many who, after leaving a role in which they had been performing well, leave a vacant role which needs to be filled by more than one person. Either the role is discovered to be too large for a new incumbent and is simply split into two or, more probably, parts of the job's tasks are given to other colleagues. Can you imagine working so hard in a role that it transpires that you are genuinely doing the work of more than one person? Perhaps you are such a person or one of your colleagues is.

Rather than becoming indispensable, aim to be invaluable in your role. Yes, you could be replaced but an exact hard-working clone would probably be impossible to find. The challenge is that you need your bosses to recognize this fact while you are still in the role and not only after you have vacated it. You need to work out how you can market what you are doing without it being seen to be selfish showing off. Perhaps you could – intelligently and subtly – share information about things you are doing at the appropriate moments.

Seek out opportunities beyond your remit and job description. This might entail you offering to your boss to take on extra tasks if you feel they will get you noticed and potentially seen in a more positive light. Perhaps your boss is complaining about having too little time to write a report and you could offer to draft it for him. It is always good to offer to do things that are visible, such as attend a meeting or make a presentation. At other times you might help colleagues who are struggling or have too much to do.

The secret is to work hard without actually doing two shifts, taking into account Chapter 8's advice on working in a smart way. You should not have to come into work and leave so late that you become exhausted, potentially burnt out. People who see you working like that will think you are either crazy or totally lacking in time-management skills.

ENCOURAGE OTHERS WITH WHOM YOU WORK TO 'GO THE EXTRA MILE'

Some people think that, if only they – out of all their colleagues – work harder and go the extra mile, they will stand out and will appear so special that they will excel in their career. I must admit that I may once have thought this. But the truth is that, if you can also encourage your team, your colleagues and even potentially your boss to do more than is expected of them, they might actually appreciate your help in enabling them also to be seen to be 'going the extra mile'.

I would understand if you chose not to encourage any potential rivals for future promotions in the same way. In that case, you should do all you can to stand out and be seen as the candidate who is most ready to take on a particular, more senior role.

If you manage a team, you should encourage all of your team members to get into the habit of working beyond their own job descriptions and you must make a concerted effort to acknowledge their extra work and performance. Can you imagine the outcome if you were a department head and your entire department had a reputation in your company for doing more than what was asked and expected of them?

Putting it all together

High-performing employees typically do what is expected of them really well and, most importantly, undertake and complete even more work tasks than would normally be asked of someone holding their position. You have to do the same if you wish to succeed and excel in your job. Start by understanding and doing well what is asked of you, and then, over time, start looking for and offering to do extra work. This might involve taking the burden off your boss. But be careful not to take on so much work that you have to work excessive overtime. Your aim is to work in a smart way within normal working hours and, if you cannot take on much extra, do not worry – just do what you are able to do really well. And encourage your team and perhaps some of your peers to start 'going above and beyond the call of duty' to do more than you or their bosses would expect of them.

It helps if you enjoy the work that you are doing; I could not imagine offering to do more work than was being asked of me if I found my work boring or tedious. Offer to do those extra tasks that you really enjoy doing and avoid things that you will not feel motivated to do well. If you wish to help your boss and you know he has many tasks that you could offer to help with, choose wisely what you offer to do. And remember, do not overwork and do not spend too long finishing these extra tasks and risking burning out just because you want to impress your bosses by 'going that extra mile'!

21 Work with grace and humility

> 'I believe the first test of a truly great man is in his humility.'
> John Ruskin

> 'In the course of my life, I have often had to eat my words, and I must confess that I have always found it a wholesome diet.' Winston Churchill

> 'Mistakes are always forgivable, if one has the courage to admit them.' Bruce Lee

> 'Arrogance invites ruin; humility receives benefits.' Chinese proverb

> 'No one should be ashamed to admit they are wrong, which is but saying, in other words, that they are wiser today than they were yesterday.' Alexander Pope

When was the last time you admitted to a colleague that you were wrong or had made a mistake and were willing to apologize if needed?

I have lost count of the number of colleagues with whom I have worked who seem unable to admit when they are wrong or have made a mistake. Furthermore, many of them would quite strongly maintain that what they are saying, doing or believing is right, in spite of obvious evidence or feedback to the contrary. When a leader takes such a stubborn or arrogant stand, it can have devastating consequences for an organization. A well-publicized example is the 2009 global financial crisis, which seems to have been partly the result of the misguided stubbornness and arrogance of some leaders running global banks.

You might assume that any strong-willed, determined and firm colleague or boss might lack grace and humility, but it is my experience that there are many focused and strong individuals who demonstrate amazing humility. In some cases they are the first to want to hear other points of view, to question what they are thinking and, most importantly, to admit when they might be wrong.

Humble and gracious people are willing to let go of many things which might be holding them back, for example:

- a certain belief system
- having a big ego
- fearing a loss of face
- fearing being seen as weak
- the need always to be right
- a need to win all arguments
- the need to show who is the boss.

No one is perfect and, equally, you cannot grow if you are not able to see and admit where you need to change what you are thinking, doing or saying. A genuinely humble and gracious person will normally recognize when they might be wrong about something, explore this and readily admit their mistakes before apologizing as needed.

RECOGNIZE THAT YOU ARE NOT ALWAYS RIGHT

Reflect upon your working life – when have you been right and when not? How often do you admit to yourself and to others that you may have made a mistake or done something wrong?

Ask a few of your close colleagues whether you ever come across as being stubborn and not open to other points of view, not listening to others and refusing to change a view or opinion. Explore with them whether they have ever experienced you not being willing to admit that you were wrong or had a made a mistake, and ask them whether they view you as someone who readily apologizes and admits your faults. You might ask them to start observing how you act and to let you know how you respond in those key moments, such as when faced with someone saying that you have made a mistake.

It is so important to understand that we might be exhibiting stubbornness and arrogance which we may be blind to. You might recall the earlier chapter on overcoming your blind spots. I will never forget the day that my teenage son looked me in the eye and said, 'Dad, you always think that you are right and you never listen to me. I would hate to work in your office with you.' I do hope that, if you have children, they would never think or say the same thing to you.

BECOME COMFORTABLE IN ADMITTING YOUR FAULTS

Be ready to admit your mistakes and apologize when needed. I am not suggesting that you need to appear soft and to give in at the slightest resistance to what you are doing. If there are times when you feel you are doing the right thing, you are allowed to hold firm to your principles and what you believe, even when others think you are making a mistake. Newly appointed coaches and managers of sports teams often act this way when their team might be having a losing streak.

A balance needs to be struck between holding firm and not rushing to change direction because others say you are making a mistake versus being open to hearing what others think and being ready to admit when you may have misjudged things and made incorrect choices or decisions.

Do not be like some recent banking traders. After making losses, they failed to report them and then attempted to keep trading to recoup the lost money. This created an even larger loss, which caused severe problems both for their careers and for their banking employers.

ENCOURAGE OTHERS TO BE HUMBLE

I once had a boss who loved hearing his own voice and found it very hard when others did not agree with him. It was particularly difficult when one of us suggested that what he planned to do or a decision he had made appeared to be wrong. People became afraid to challenge him and there were times when, even in the face of the facts, our boss would still deny that he might have made a mistake. One day, when I was alone with my boss, I remember asking him, 'Do you not realize that you often refuse to hear other points of view and seem determined never to admit that you might be wrong?'

Amazingly, after that one conversation my boss did begin to change, and he actually asked me to warn him if I noticed that he was becoming blind to his own lack of openness and humility. Just a simple conversation enabled a person to see things differently. I challenge you to be brave enough, when necessary, to have a similar conversation with any colleague or boss.

Putting it all together

Learn to become like Britain's wartime Prime Minister, Winston Churchill, who found that moments of having to be humble and 'eat his own words' were invaluable. I am sure that he would never have wanted to hide from such moments by stubbornly refusing to acknowledge the truth.

Readily admit your faults and mistakes and then learn from them. I recognize that there may be times when it is embarrassing to admit something openly, and in some parts of the world this can result in a serious loss of face, particularly if you are in a management position. In those situations it is quite common to admit things only to your boss in private. The key is that you must be honest with yourself and not be in denial. Ask colleagues to let you know when you are being too stubborn or narrow-minded and at risk of making a serious mistake.

People will value more highly a colleague or boss who will admit that he/she is human and can make mistakes. Such humble people also develop more empathy and understanding of others and are less likely to get angry and emotional every time one of their own team or a colleague makes a mistake.

22 Work quickly when necessary

> 'The world is moving so fast these days that the man who says it can't be done is generally interrupted by someone doing it.'
> Elbert Hubbard

> 'If everything seems under control, you're just not going fast enough.' Mario Andretti

> 'I cannot work fast enough.' Werner Herzog

> 'If you fall behind, run faster. Never give up, never surrender, and rise up against the odds.' Jesse Jackson

> 'If my doctor told me I had only six minutes to live, I wouldn't brood. I'd type a little faster.' Isaac Asimov

We all talk about being busy, being in a hurry and never having enough time. Everywhere we look in the workplace, tasks need completing by specific deadlines and we rarely feel that we are given enough time. So much of our work can be called time-dependent, meaning that the work is of little or no value if it is not completed within a certain time frame. Examples include:

- a sales forecast due to be completed by tomorrow
- a client quotation needed today
- a change in a production line that has to be made within an hour
- updating database software by the end of the month.

The challenge is compounded by information overload, with too much information needing to be filtered and dealt with in too little time. An obvious example is the large number of emails that most of us send and receive on a daily basis. I recently coached someone who works with a large Silicon Valley-based company who had over 4,000 unread emails in her work inbox. She seems to spend a large part of her day rapidly skim reading hundreds of emails and then quickly responding to the key ones.

As I have coached hundreds of individuals in the workplace, I have discovered that we waste precious time by delaying and procrastinating. We might know that the work is urgent and important but we still find ourselves being slow to start the task. The result is that we end up with even less time to complete something that has to be finished by a certain deadline.

PACE YOURSELF

When we are in the gym on a running, rowing or step machine, we normally pace ourselves and do not spend the entire 20- or 30-minute workout time exercising at high speed – we would become too exhausted before our workout had finished. Likewise, when working, if we were to spend the entire day rushing and working on every task as quickly as physically possible, we would burn out and become unproductive. I am sure that there are exceptions, but most people function more optimally when they vary the speed and intensity at which they work during the day.

In writing this book, I work in short, fast bursts, typing quickly for perhaps 30 or 45 minutes before standing up and having a break.

I encourage you to watch consciously how you work and to pace yourself. It is also helpful to know when in the working day you might be most productive and comfortable working in a fast and intense way. I work best in the mornings and in the evenings. As a result, I like to start work early and work in a fast and intensive way for two to three hours before having a calmer midday through to the late afternoon.

Such pacing will help you to avoid burn-out and will enable you to focus your energy on those tasks which you must complete quickly.

CHOOSE CAREFULLY THE WORK YOU WILL UNDERTAKE QUICKLY

There is a time and a place for everything – including working very quickly. The secret is to use your judgement in deciding when to put in the effort to work especially quickly. To enable you to decide when you will work faster than normal, here are some key questions to consider:

- When is speed more important than precise accuracy or extra details?
- Are you needing to catch up with others or are you behind schedule?
- Are you competing with others and needing to complete something before somebody else does?
- Are you wishing to stay ahead of others?
- When is it important to finish something quickly to impress your boss?

With experience, we all become more proficient at using our skills of discernment – of knowing when to increase our workflow and our speed of working. If you always choose to work quickly, be aware that people will become used to such fast working and this can have two downsides for how you are perceived. Firstly, they may come to expect this of you and may feel that you are being too slow when you work in a slower and probably more normal way. Secondly, your boss and colleagues may become so used to your keenness to work quickly that they stop recognizing and acknowledging this as a strength of yours.

IMPRESS YOUR BOSS AND SENIOR COLLEAGUES WITH YOUR FAST WORK

To be able to truly excel in the workplace, your work needs to be noticed by those bosses and senior colleagues who have an influence on your career and possible future promotions. I am not suggesting that you blatantly show off but I am suggesting that sometimes, when you have rushed to complete tasks which are very important, you should be ready to let others know.

There will be times when you will need to stay longer in the office – in the evenings, coming in very early in the morning or spending weekends at work – or will need to take work home in order to complete something quickly. It is a shame if key people do not realize how committed you are to completing the work as quickly as possible. Let them know what you are doing so that you feel your effort will not go unnoticed. Some individuals might like to announce loudly how they completed some important work quickly while others might wish to be more indirect and subtle in how they share what they have been doing.

Putting it all together

We live in a world in which everything seems to be needed now and working quickly is normally viewed as a positive attribute in the workplace. However, unless you really have to, I would not suggest that you do all of your work as quickly as possible if this entails excessive overtime and the risk of burning out and becoming too stressed.

Someone manning a call centre telephone where all customer complaints need to be dealt with within a couple of minutes is in quite a different situation from someone working on a farm, where much of the work is spread over many days.

You are encouraged to follow a combination of the three strategies that I have shared in this chapter in a way that works for your unique work situation. Do not let yourself become too frazzled and stressed by doing everything at high speed – remember to pace yourself and to be selective in choosing when to work very quickly. And, finally, be conscious of how you seek to be noticed and acknowledged for when you have worked extra fast.

23 Reduce your stress levels

> 'Tension is who you think you should be. Relaxation is who you are.' Chinese proverb

> 'It makes no sense to worry about things you have no control over because there's nothing you can do about them, and why worry about things you do control? The activity of worrying keeps you immobilized.' Wayne Dyer

> 'I promise you nothing is as chaotic as it seems. Nothing is worth your health. Nothing is worth poisoning yourself into stress, anxiety, and fear.' Steve Maraboli

> 'If you are distressed by anything external, the pain is not due to the thing itself, but to your estimate of it; and this you have the power to revoke at any moment.' Marcus Aurelius

> 'The more tranquil a man becomes, the greater is his success, his influence, his power for good. Calmness of mind is one of the beautiful jewels of wisdom.' James Allen

Nobody can truly excel at work if their time spent in the workplace gives them regular or ongoing levels of stress. Some might say that this is the price that must be paid for success but I would respond that if stress is part of what constitutes 'success', that definition is wrong.

It is rare to meet somebody who never gets stressed or anxious when they are at work. I observe levels of stress and anxiety constantly on the increase across the organizations with which I work. So many of today's employers are streamlining and laying off people, expecting higher levels of productivity, and wanting people to multitask and attend meetings while also completing all their other tasks.

Stress and anxiety affect our mood, our productivity, our ability to interact with others and, most worryingly, our health – physical, emotional, mental and spiritual. Once our health is affected, our future long-term willingness and ability to excel in the workplace can be greatly reduced. Evidence shows that high and sustained levels of workplace stress can lead to heart attacks, strokes and other life-threatening illnesses.

We become stressed when our lives are not in what is called 'the flow', when life is not flowing in a comfortable way and we need to resist what is happening or feel unable to accept it. A lot of work-related stress comes from being uncomfortable, unhappy and/or resisting what is being asked of us – perhaps feeling uncomfortable with what our new boss is asking us to do, resisting working overtime or having tasks that are particularly difficult to complete successfully.

One challenge of trying to reduce stress levels is that you first have to recognize that you are stressed – and in what ways. Each of us seems to have different tolerance levels: you might have a situation of two people with identical work, where one of the two is extremely stressed and showing physical signs – such as backache, trouble sleeping or breathing difficulties – while the other seems to show no physical signs of stress or anxiety at all.

RECOGNIZE THE SIGNS OF YOUR OWN STRESS

Self-awareness is key, and knowing how stress might be affecting you is essential as a first step before you can plan how to reduce your stress levels. In what ways might you be showing signs of stress? Here is a checklist to help you explore how you might be exhibiting symptoms.

Signs of stress

Symptom	✓	Symptom	✓
Being depressed		Backache	
Acting irritably		Muscle pains and aches	
Sleeping difficulties		Feeling uninterested and demotivated about work	
Suffering from fatigue		Not wishing to connect with others and socialize	
Feeling anxious		Becoming angry and upset too easily	
Panic attacks		Not loving and caring for those around you	
Lacking concentration		Different eating and drinking habits	
Stomachache and cramps		Headaches and blurred vision	

This list is not exhaustive and signs of stress are unique to each of us. If you notice that you are exhibiting any possible signs of stress, you should start trying to relieve your symptoms immediately. This might involve taking sleeping pills to help you sleep better or visiting a chiropractor to help relieve your tight shoulders or back pain. But do understand that these actions are only ways of reducing the *effects* of stress and I would strongly encourage you to explore how you can eliminate the *root causes* of any stress in your life. If something in your work or workplace is causing you to feel stressed, you should try to change it. I have helped many leaders and their teams to reduce their levels of stress, and the most commonly needed actions can be quite major and might involve a person needing to change what they do in order to work fewer hours, to work with nicer colleagues or with a better boss or to a job that is more aligned with their natural strengths and interests.

MAKE EXTRA EFFORT TO SURVIVE A STRESSFUL WORK ENVIRONMENT

In an ideal world, the perfect method of eliminating stress from our lives would be to remove ourselves from the cause(s) of that stress. In reality, though, very few people have the freedom to walk away from their work and careers and I am not suggesting that you take such drastic action, particularly when you might, without consciously realizing it, only attract similar work or home situations into your life.

I recognize that the main source of stress for people relates to their job and that most of us are not in a position to be able to change jobs easily in order to find less stressful work and workplace environments. As a result, we need to ask ourselves how we can reduce our levels of stress when we might need to stay in a stressful job and workplace. There are many possible ways, but here are some key suggestions for you to consider:

- Relax and try to avoid continually thinking about work problems and negative issues. Attempt not to take work home, even in the form of complaining or moaning about work issues.
- Exercise your body as often as possible. Perhaps take the stairs instead of the elevator, try to join a nearby gym and endeavour to go at least every other day.
- Do not sit for too long at your desk working at the computer and, if you must, try to have your company buy you an ergonomic chair that is good for your back and for your posture.
- Eat and drink as healthily as possible. If you are addicted to your morning coffee, try to make it only one cup rather than three. When we are stressed, we can sometimes forget to eat and to drink, so remind yourself to eat on a regular basis and try to drink water all through the day.
- I also encourage you to learn from some of the other chapters in this book, such as Chapter 4 on learning to say no, and to be more assertive about your own needs.

HELP OTHERS TO REDUCE THEIR STRESS LEVELS

There is nothing healthy or positive about having to work among stressed colleagues. Their stress can sometimes feel contagious and bring you down too. Furthermore, a team cannot hope to excel if team members are burdened by stress. And beware those who preach that some stress can be a healthy way of pushing people to work harder!

Encourage others to recognize their own levels and symptoms of stress, and help them eliminate or at least reduce the causes of their stress. You might achieve this through walking your talk and being seen to be calmer and more relaxed than you used to be.

Putting it all together

Stress can be a killer and it is far too prevalent in today's workplaces. You may not die because of stress but stress can easily kill your energy levels, motivation, relationships, health and mindset. Recognizing how stress might be affecting you may not be easy and you might be tempted to ignore or deny some of the signs, but I urge you to persist and truly understand how you might be living under stress. It might be the stress of long work hours, of realizing that your 'to-do' list is getting too long or of having a long commute to and from work every day. The possible causes of stress are varied and each of us reacts to the same things in quite different ways.

Adopt habits and activities which can counter and reduce the effects of stress and help you to be more relaxed and healthy. In the longer term you might need to consider moving away from the sources of the stress, and this might entail seeking a new job or career.

Without recognizing and reducing your workplace stress, it will be hard for you to ever truly feel that you are excelling in your job and career. In the short term you might be pleasing your boss, having great relationships with your colleagues and even being promoted very quickly, but the stress you feel inside will be slowly destroying your potential to continue excelling.

24 Work on your career plan

> 'Good plans shape good decisions. That's why good planning helps to make elusive dreams come true.' Geoffrey Fisher

> 'Think ahead. Don't let day-to-day operations drive out planning.' Donald Rumsfeld

> 'I am a big believer in visualization. I run through my races mentally so that I feel even more prepared.' Allyson Felix

> 'Plans are only good intentions unless they immediately degenerate into hard work.' Peter Drucker

> 'You have brains in your head. You have feet in your shoes. You can steer yourself any direction you choose. You're on your own. And you know what you know. And YOU are the one who'll decide where to go...' Dr Seuss

I spent a decade in the recruitment industry and must have interviewed several thousand candidates over that time. Over 90 per cent of these job-seekers were looking for new jobs because they were either in or had recently left jobs in which they were unable to perform really well. However, most were never really able to answer what seemed the obvious question: 'What kind of job or career are you now seeking in which you will be able to perform really well and where you will be content and enjoy the demands of the work?' So often, these job-seeking candidates were looking for similar jobs to their previous ones but with a higher salary.

You will not consistently excel in your work if you only seek more remuneration. Furthermore, if you have not succeeded in a role to date and you choose to move into a similar role, what makes you think that you will perform any better and finally excel? This brings to mind a quote attributed to Einstein:

> *'Insanity is doing the same thing over and over again but expecting different results.'*

I have had many friends, family members and work colleagues who have spent years working in jobs that they admit to finding boring or unenjoyable or in which they are not performing well. When I challenge them by asking why they don't change what they are doing, their response is normally similar: 'But I have no idea what to do or how to do it.'

A simple answer is to have a plan. Once you have written a plan and got going, you will be surprised how things happen to help you achieve it – it is almost as if a plan focuses your awareness and opens your eyes to things that could help you achieve your aims.

Having career clarity can help you optimize your performance in your current work, because now you will know that it is part of a bigger picture. So, even if your present job is a bit tedious, boring or difficult, you can identify what you need to achieve in it and how long you need to do it for in order to help you achieve your longer-term career goals.

KNOW YOUR CAREER DESTINATION OR GOALS

Where are you wishing to head with your work and career? Too many people in the working world are guilty of what Lewis Carroll put so succinctly:

> *'If you don't know where you are going, any road will get you there.'*

Building on the first three chapters of this book, in which I asked you to explore your dreams and passions, your potential blind spots and your strengths and weaknesses, I advise you to start mapping out a career plan. The first step is to understand what your career and life goals are. You can make a good start by exploring your answers to the following question: in a perfect world, what would your ideal job role be and where would you like to be working in three, five and ten years' time?

Your career and work goals ought to be in harmony or alignment with your overall life goals and the goals of your partner and family. It may not be ideal if your career goals involve switching to a lower-paid job when your spouse has a goal that you both pay off a house loan as quickly as possible. At a minimum, reach an understanding about your career goals with the important people in your personal life. If you do not all agree on where you would like to head with your career, at least agree to disagree and over time to work through any differences of opinion.

PLAN HOW YOU WILL TRAVEL TO YOUR CAREER DESTINATION

Now is the time to make a plan of how you will move yourself from where you are today to where you wish to be. You should create a plan which maps out over time what activities and actions you should undertake to help you move your career in an optimal direction. For some this might involve a lot of change and uncertainty; for others it might simply mean staying in a current job role and working to be promoted. There are some very contented people who are happy to remain in their current role for their entire working lives.

Here are some ideas of what you might need to consider as you draft your career plan:

- Are you in the right role for you today? If so, what do you need to learn and master in this job to help you move forward?
- Are you with the ideal employer today? If so, do you need to work to gain promotions or will you plan to move on to another organization? Which option is better for your career? You may not be sure and, if in doubt, I would advise you to stay with the company that you know well.

- Do you need to learn new skills through studying? Would you do this as self-study, part-time study on a course or do you need or wish to stop work at some point to study full-time?
- Are there bigger potential changes required in your ideal career plan? These might include taking early retirement, moving to part-time working, becoming self-employed or even moving countries.

BE READY TO MAKE BRAVE CHOICES

A plan is only a plan until you actually start putting it into action and I know that, for some of you, this might involve making some difficult choices. The majority of people feel that they are not in an ideal job which uses their strengths and in which they feel fulfilled. As a result, most people's career plans include a need to move on from their current jobs. This is not easy and, as we discussed in the chapter on embracing and accepting change, most people would rather stay in a sub-optimal situation that feels safe than move to an optimal one.

If you are not in the right job for you today, you must be ready to make the brave decision to resign and move on to a new job, and possibly into a new field for you.

Putting it all together

The best way of ensuring that you will be able to excel over the remaining years of your working life is to have a plan of where you want your career to go. This plan should encompass an idea of the roles that would be best aligned to your strengths, passions and dreams.

It is not easy to create a career plan. Often, a plan is a work in progress which you can revise and develop over time as you become clearer about what it is that you wish to achieve and in what kinds of roles you wish to work. It may be that you simply plan where you might like to be in five years' time (for example, in your boss's job) and beyond that you may have no idea of what you wish to do. It is better to have a five-year goal than no goals at all, and any goals that you set for your working life are at least partly aimed at enabling you to work with your strengths and passions. I do realize that you may have other goals – the main one being to earn a certain level of remuneration – but you can plan to bring all of your goals together, such as aiming to be in a high-paying role in the career field that you feel is best suited to you and your dreams.

25 Work on your judgement and discernment

❝ *'Good judgement comes from experience. Experience comes from bad judgement.'* Anon.

❝ *'Don't fight a battle if you don't gain anything by winning.'* Field Marshal Erwin Rommel

❝ *'Failure is not a single, cataclysmic event. You don't fail overnight. Instead, failure is a few errors in judgement, repeated every day.'* Jim Rohn

❝ *'We need discernment in what we see and what we hear and what we believe.'* Charles R. Swindoll

❝ *'Greatness lies not in being strong, but in the right use of strength.'* Henry Ward Beecher

Success in the workplace frequently involves needing to spot and seize opportunities, something that is often described as being entrepreneurial. Having the insight to see possibilities and then to choose optimally between options can be called having good judgement and discernment.

Judgement is aligned to the process of decision-making, which is the subject of a later chapter, but judgement is not so much a process as it is a combination of learned experiences, intuition and gut feeling. It could be described as how a person applies their wisdom to situations. It is about making the ideal choices in any situation. There are times when you are presented with information and opinions and then you must make a decision based on your experience and gut feeling. The first quote above, stating that judgement comes from experience, sums up my view that judgement cannot be easily taught – although we can learn from observing cases of good and bad judgement.

Judgement and discernment have similar meanings, but discernment is about being able to see what is really happening and to see the true nature of things. I view discernment as a foundation for judgement. As we gain years of work experience, our skills of discernment and judgement improve, and these skills are much valued by organizations in their more senior staff and leaders.

On the opposite side, organizations may be wary of people who do not demonstrate these skills. The person who seems to lack both good judgement and discernment is the kind of employee who will make too many mistakes, and will often repeat those same mistakes. The ideal is that we genuinely learn from the mistakes and poor decisions we make during our working lives and, over time, our levels of judgement and discernment will improve.

In the working world we rarely have enough time and resources to do everything that we want or need to achieve. This makes the need to judge vital to ensuring that our valuable time and resources are not wasted, and we must learn to become more discerning in everything that we do, including who we delegate work to or who we involve in a particular project.

LEARN FROM YOUR OWN MISTAKES AND MISJUDGEMENTS

Too many people fail to recognize their own mistakes and moments of poor judgement or lack of discernment. In Chapter 2, on knowing and fixing your blind spots, we explored how this is common in many people. You cannot demonstrate great judgement and discernment without having sufficient wisdom and experience. Wisdom only comes from observing and learning from all your life and work experiences. To gain true wisdom, you must be fully aware of and willing to learn from everything you do, particularly when you have made a mistake.

Ask yourself, 'How could I have done things differently?' or 'In the future what could I do differently?' You may have heard the saying that your best teacher is your last mistake.

In addition, avoid the common habit of blaming others and never yourself when things do not go as you wanted or as planned. This is a sure way of never truly learning from your mistakes.

Finally, if you struggle to know when and how you might be making mistakes and exhibiting poor judgement, ask a trusted work colleague for their opinions and insights.

JUDGE OTHERS WELL AND OBJECTIVELY

If you wish to increase your chances of failing in your work, then a good place to start is to judge people poorly or incorrectly. In essence, this means jumping to incorrect assumptions and demonstrating a lack of understanding about how people act, think and interact.

If you can develop wisdom in all matters relating to people, you can truly stand out among your peers. The secret is to form opinions and views about somebody that are based on what the person is really like and those views may well change as you spend more time working with the person. It is not easy for us to change our opinions of people and of their work, particularly as we live in a world in which jumping to conclusions and forming opinions based on first impressions are commonplace. The other parties will not feel understood, valued or listened to by you if they feel you are misjudging them.

Good judgement revolves around one's own opinions and conclusions, so avoid becoming biased and too influenced by other people's opinions and views. Do not blindly agree when others say something like, 'He is always so lazy and doesn't care', 'She hates details and never reads my reports' or 'He only works here because no other department will have him.'

Develop the skills of good judgement and discernment before you ever have to start recruiting, evaluating and promoting people. If you don't, you risk making costly mistakes in your choices of who you hire and promote.

SEEK EXPERIENCES TO DEVELOP YOUR WISDOM

If you have been in the same role for a long time and have been doing the same tasks, you might benefit from some change. This could be achieved through seeking a new role in your organization or being involved with some ad hoc projects. Taking on new or additional responsibilities can be an excellent way to gain wisdom from the variety of new issues, decisions and challenges that you will face. As well as strengthening your skills of judgement and discernment, this additional work exposure can give you more visibility and increase your promotion prospects.

Putting it all together

The skills of good judgement and discernment are rarely discussed as essential criteria for success, but they are truly indispensable. During a normal working day, we all continually need to make choices and decisions – some are small and some are large and we can so easily make the wrong calls if we lack sufficient judgement and discernment.

This book contains 50 varied secrets, some of which might seem contradictory – for example, being patient and working quickly. It is through using your skills of judgement and discernment that you will be able to decide which of these secrets you should follow at different moments in your working day.

I have chosen the 50 secrets given here using my own judgement and discernment. I hope that you will use your own unique judgement to decide which of them are applicable to you and which are essential.

Using good judgement and discernment enables us to demonstrate our own uniqueness in the workplace. Everything we do reflects our unique choices – no two authors could ever create identical lists of 50 secrets of work success because our lives and experiences are too varied to allow this to happen.

26 Work on your body language and presence

‘ *'With me it's always about first impressions.'* Billy Zane

‘ *'You can tell a lot by someone's body language.'* Harvey Wolter

‘ *'I have three tools at my disposal – my whistle, my body language and my talk. It is a question of how I marry them up to try to get the players around to my way of thinking.'* Alan Lewis

‘ *'You will never make a good impression on other people until you stop thinking about what sort of impression you are making. Even in literature and art, no man who bothers about originality will ever be original.'* C. S. Lewis

‘ *'We convince by our presence.'* Walt Whitman

How often do you judge people by their appearance and how they present themselves when you first meet them? Do you spot their crumpled shirt, laddered tights and dirty shoes and then form an opinion about that person? Or do you perhaps see their stooped posture, a nervous and limp handshake and mumbling self-introduction before you form an opinion? Either way, I am sure that you are like most people who form impressions and views of other people in the first few seconds of meeting them.

I spent more than ten years working as a recruiter and during those years I will have spent on average 45 minutes interviewing each of perhaps 5,000 job-seekers. I came to realize that my first impressions of each candidate and the opinions I reached at the end of each interview were often in alignment – weak candidates did not give good first impressions while stronger candidates actually did give better first impressions.

It is so important that how we come across when we are with other people is how we want to be seen and perceived. Ideally, you should make the effort to present yourself in the best possible way and to be memorable – somebody whom others will want to work and connect with.

How we come across involves both visible and non-visible elements. The visible elements include such factors as how we dress, how we walk and stand, where we focus our eyes when we speak, how cleanly cut and shaven we are and what kind of make-up we might wearing. The non-visible elements are partly linked to the visible ones and might include how confident, nervous, arrogant or happy we appear. It is quite possible to dress and act very professionally or confidently but still give other people the opposite impression, because we have unconsciously revealed that we are in fact uncomfortable in the formal suit or dress that we are wearing.

FIRST IMPRESSIONS DO COUNT

Here are some key tips on how to make a memorable and positive lasting first impression on anyone you meet or connect with. This advice is equally appropriate to all of the interactions you have, even with colleagues you know well.

I cannot advise you on what you wear in terms of clothes, shoes, accessories and hair style and so on, except to say that you should feel comfortable in your choice and it should be professional enough for the work environment you are in – for example, someone working in an investment bank might need to appear more formal than someone working for a food manufacturer. I always like to remind those I coach of the adage 'When in Rome, do as the Romans do.' Look at those around you and consider copying and mimicking some of your successful colleagues or bosses in how they dress and act.

In addition to mastering how you dress, here are some of the essential must-dos for you to follow:

- Always look at the person with whom you are communicating face to face, even when you are talking over video conference or Skype. People feel very uncomfortable when another person avoids eye contact and they might assume that you are nervous, uncomfortable or have something to hide.
- Have an upright posture when sitting or standing, keeping your shoulders back, and avoid appearing to slump over with a rounded back. Good posture projects confidence and is as important to remember when you are sitting as when you are standing.
- Make your handshake confident and firm while keeping eye contact; allow others to pass through doorways before you; wait until asked before sitting and, when sitting, do not fidget and move around too much.

Be aware of how others are acting with you and copy them as needed, for instance only taking off your jacket after others in a meeting have done so. This imitating happens naturally, often without us realizing it and is called 'postural congruence'. It is useful to be conscious of this, noticing how people copy each other unawares much of the time – in a meeting people might cross their legs or their arms almost simultaneously.

Be aware of cultural differences, norms and expectations. Cultural norms and taboos vary widely. As examples, in many parts of the world you should never ask a woman to shake your hand, you must not sit showing the sole of your shoe, and you must not touch the other person.

AVOID BAD HABITS AND POTENTIAL ODDITIES

Be aware of any bad habits that you have which may give a bad impression to others when they meet you. The possible list of such habits is probably endless, but here are some examples of things you might want to do to guarantee making a good impression on others: do not bite your nails, polish your shoes, do not wear tights with ladders in them, avoid clothes with missing buttons, remove food from your teeth, keep your jacket on to hide any armpit sweat stains, wear perfume or deodorant if you risk smelling and, last but not least for men, be clean-shaven.

We are all unique and some people love dyeing their hair orange, having tattoos, wearing three studs in each ear or wearing unusual clothes. Understand that such unique statements might not be appropriate to help you succeed in your work environment and you must decide how willing you are to compromise. To excel at work, you need to make others feel comfortable with you and have confidence in you and, rightly or wrongly, people have their own biases, values and opinions. At weekends be yourself 100 per cent but, when you are at work, be ready to tone something down or hide some of your individuality, such as a large tattoo on your arm.

ACT PROFESSIONALLY

As a final must-do, once you have mastered how you are physically presenting yourself, project a mindset and attitude which match the professional and modern way in which you are trying to dress and act. What might this mean? Perhaps you would benefit from trying to project more confidence, being calmer and more poised, having a positive charisma, being more relaxed and smiling more often.

Putting it all together

Sadly, people make judgements and decisions about other people based in part on how they present themselves and how they look. This might be appropriate but could be viewed as discriminatory. However, this is the reality and it is unlikely to change, especially given our increasing workload, which leave us less time to get to know each other and therefore more reliant on those first impressions.

The advice in this chapter is essentially saying look at yourself in the mirror and be comfortable that what you see is ideal for the work environment in which you are employed. If in doubt, seek the advice of others including trusted colleagues.

You may choose to completely change your wardrobe and to work on your posture. No matter what changes you choose to make in how you come across to others, I implore you to please be honest and authentic. If you cannot really be yourself in a certain workplace and you feel you are having to continually act or are being fake, then seriously consider finding a new and more aligned work environment in which to work.

27 Be a great learner

> 'Live as if you were to die tomorrow. Learn as if you were to live forever.' Mahatma Gandhi

> 'I am always ready to learn although I do not always like being taught.' Winston Churchill

> 'Being ignorant is not so much a shame, as being unwilling to learn.' Benjamin Franklin

> 'If you can't explain it simply, you don't understand it well enough.' Albert Einstein

> 'Learning is what most adults will do for a living in the 21st century.' Alfred Edward Perlman

I recall a conversation with my grandmother in which, after I had qualified as an accountant, I announced that I had finished studying, to which she responded that successful people never stop learning and relearning. After nearly 25 years in the working world, I know her words to be true and would go even further in saying that learning is power and that acquiring and correctly applying knowledge in your work are essential in enabling you to stand out among your peers and to excel.

We now live in a world where none of us can stand still and stop seeking and learning, and where knowledge is a competitive advantage, for organizations as well as for individuals. I recently saw the results of a study showing that half of what is learned in the first year of various college degree courses is no longer relevant and has been superseded by the time of the student's graduation. In every profession and career there is a constant stream of new information, ideas, processes and ideas, none of which can be ignored if you wish to continue performing well and excelling in your job. It is true, regardless of whether you are an accountant, a police officer, a civil servant, a plumber, an electronics engineer, a chef or a nurse.

Learning can take many forms, from simply learning on the job through to attending full-time courses. No matter how you learn, the key is to have a learning mindset that is open to new things and humble enough to recognize that there may be many things that you do not know well.

Most organizations understand all of this and, because of their demand, the training and learning sector has grown into a multi-billion dollar industry. As a result, you can be spoilt for choice when seeking to learn and improve yourself. The following strategies will help you make the right choices and ensure that you get what you need.

HAVE CLEAR LEARNING GOALS

Do you know what you need to learn and be trained in to ensure that your personal toolbox of skills, knowledge and behaviours is optimally filled up? As part of an annual performance evaluation or review with your boss, have you agreed some goals or have you been invited by your company to attend particular training? Only you are able to draw up a clear picture of your needs and, in order to ensure this, I suggest that you carry out a needs analysis to identify any gaps that may exist in your skills, knowledge and behaviours. A gap is the difference between where you are now and the optimal set of skills you need to succeed in your current role and also to be able to perform in roles into which you hope to be promoted.

There are two key ways of discovering what gaps may exist:

- You can seek the views of your boss and colleagues.
- You can observe high-performing and senior colleagues to understand how they are performing well and to see what you may need to acquire or do to emulate or surpass them.

Remember that you can acquire knowledge and skills in many ways, including by attending conferences, trade shows, workshops and courses. You can also acquire them through learning on the job, seeking job rotations, asking for extra involvement in work projects and activities, work travel overseas to gain new exposures, reading relevant journals, books or websites, speaking with senior mentors and finding the help of an executive coach.

BE PROACTIVE AND ASSERTIVE WITH YOUR HR COLLEAGUES

Ask for and demand relevant training and learning experiences. Perhaps you need to request approval to attend an industry conference or to attend a business school course. This might involve you having to be quite assertive with your HR or training-focused colleagues. If you work in a small organization lacking HR support, you may have to make the request of your boss or company owner. As well as requesting the money and time for such activities, you are, more importantly, seeking your colleagues' acceptance and understanding of your learning and development needs. In a nutshell, you are seeking to be valued and to have your growth needs valued. This can be more easily achieved in a working culture which supports learning but, sadly, learning cultures are not as common as they ought to be.

You may need to compromise with your HR colleagues and boss – they might ask you to delay any training until later, or they might offer alternative options. You must decide whether such compromises are acceptable or whether you might need to push back and hold firm with your initial requests.

On-the-job experience is key but only optimal if you are in the ideal job that can give you the experience needed to grow. There may be times when you will request a lateral job move in order to give you some job experience which you feel you need to enable you to better succeed in your career. As an example, I once took a role as a finance manager in the Dominican Republic in order to gain experience of being involved in a greenfield manufacturing start-up.

START READING

On average, we all read less than our parents and grandparents did. When we do read, we seem to do so in short bursts, often jumping between articles on the web rather than reading an entire book.

However, for you to absorb new ideas and knowledge, it is often necessary to read an entire book or manual and to reflect and make notes while you read. Simply to rely on other people telling or showing you may not be enough for you to understand certain details and connections between things. When I am training others, I ask my course participants to read a particular manual or book that I have written or prepared before they attend my workshops. Participants then come having gained a full picture and I can help them walk through and explore key parts, answering all their queries and concerns.

Putting it all together

Develop a learning mindset of continually learning and acquiring new ideas and knowledge while always being ready to throw away things that you thought were needed or were true but are then superseded. In this way you can hope to stay one step ahead of your peers and colleagues and be ready to excel at any challenges thrown at you.

Determining what you need to learn, train in and develop is not easy and will involve you obtaining a variety of feedback as well as analysing your own needs. If in doubt about the possible value of a particular learning or training activity, do it – it is better to over-learn than to remain ignorant.

It is as important to be ready to unlearn as it is to learn. So many of us think we know how to do things without realizing that there may be newer best-practice ways which, if we fail to understand and adopt them, might see us fall behind others. The accounting field in which I began my career is a case in point: the need to unlearn old ways and learn new ones has become essential for any accountant aspiring to reach or remain at the top of their profession.

Your decision to read and explore this book is a fantastic example of your willingness to learn and I commend you. But what do you really need to know and do better? After reading this entire book, carry out your learning needs or gap analysis and determine what else you need to do to fill any gaps.

28 Become an avid listener

> 'I like to listen. I have learned a great deal from listening carefully. Most people never listen.' Ernest Hemingway

> 'Wisdom is the reward you get for a lifetime of listening when you'd have preferred to talk.' Doug Larson

> 'If you make listening and observation your occupation, you will gain much more than you can by talk.' Robert Baden-Powell

> 'So when you are listening to somebody, completely, attentively, then you are listening not only to the words, but also to the feeling of what is being conveyed, to the whole of it, not part of it.' Jiddu Krishnamurti

> 'You cannot truly listen to anyone and do anything else at the same time.' M. Scott Peck

'Are they listening to me?' 'I never feel understood.' 'My boss never listens when I speak to him.' 'When I was presenting, people seemed more interested in their phones.'

Do these kinds of thoughts and comments sound familiar? I have never met anyone who would admit to truly being heard and understood 100 per cent of the time. In today's working world I think we are losing our listening skills due to the overload of sound, words and information that is available through all types of media and on the Internet. We might hear all that is around us, but we are failing to truly listen and to understand.

How well do you listen? Do people ever have to check that you are listening? Or, worse still, might they accuse you of not having heard what they were trying to say?

As a child, I was always told that we were born to listen rather than to speak. When I asked why, I would be told because we are born with two ears and two eyes but with only one mouth. At school I was also taught that we should seek first to understand then be understood.

Listening is a combination of both hearing what someone else is communicating and being able to acknowledge what you are hearing. In other words, listeners are not passive and good listening involves some form of response, be it a nod of your head, saying thank you or giving a more detailed reply. It is not enough to think that you listen well; the only true measure of your listening skills is if those communicating with you know that you are listening.

Listening can happen in many forms and venues and one could argue that we are listening every minute that we are awake – sometimes to our own thoughts and bodies and at other times to other people and to what is happening around us. Listening to others occurs throughout the working day in meetings, in the corridor, on the shop floor or during telephone calls, and you might be listening to one individual or to a group. A key question to ask, though, is when are we consciously and optimally listening?

PAUSE BEFORE YOU SPEAK

If you observe your colleagues when they are in conversation, you will see that most of the time they jump in to speak while the other person is still speaking or has just finished saying something, without leaving even a second's gap. Even worse, there are times when someone starts speaking before the other has even finished, which can seem quite rude. You will also have experienced someone saying something that may have had no connection with what was just said by others, leaving the impression that the last speaker had ignored what others had said. I sometimes sense that too many people speak for the sake of it and rarely give time to think deeply about what they might say.

You may be fortunate enough to watch someone who only says something after a few moments or seconds of quiet reflection, and they may just say, 'Good point' or 'You summed it up well.' Such people tend to exhibit more wisdom and they are people with whom we like to speak. You can emulate them by learning to WAIT & STOP, where these words are acronyms for two really useful reminders whenever you are in a discussion or conversation:

W = Why   **S** = Stop (pause)

A = Am   **T** = Think (think about what you have heard)

I = I   **O** = Options (reflect on what you might contribute)

T = Talking?   **P** = Proceed (speak if you need to, or stay silent)

Remembering these acronyms will help you hear and digest what has been said and show others that you have been listening. As a result, what you then say should intelligently flow from what you have heard.

PARAPHRASE AND SUMMARIZE WHAT YOU ARE HEARING

Most people like to be heard and to be valued, and they feel really appreciated when people make an effort to show that they are being heard, even if those listening might not agree with what is being communicated.

An excellent way of showing someone that you are listening to them is to make sure after they have spoken that you heard what they thought they were telling you. This is best done through summarizing, clarifying and paraphrasing what you have heard by saying something such as:

- 'Allow me to summarize what I am hearing…'
- 'If I understand correctly, what you are saying is that…'
- 'If I heard you correctly, you are trying to explain…'
- 'Am I right in what I think you are asking?…'
- 'What I am hearing is…'

As well as allowing the speaker to clarify what they are saying and to feel that you are interested, these types of question also allow you to reflect and think before speaking.

VISIBLY SHOW THAT YOU ARE LISTENING

Perception is so important and, even if you might be an expert at multitasking and be quite capable of listening to someone while you send someone an SMS, sign some papers or leaf through a file, the other party might think you are not interested in them and what they have to say.

If you wish to be a valued colleague and business partner, you must develop the habit of enabling others to sense that you are giving their words and ideas your full attention. Here are some tips on how you can ensure that you are totally present and listening when others are speaking to you:

- Maintain eye contact with those who are speaking but without staring.
- Do not move around and fidget or look distracted in any way.
- If you know you have a short concentration span, it might be good to interrupt the speaker from time to time to ask clarifying questions.
- If you must do something, do it thoughtfully. For example, if you wish to make notes on what is being said, do so by looking up at the person and down at the paper you are writing on or the tablet you are typing into. Do not just look at the paper or tablet without making eye contact with the speaker.
- Respond to what is being said in non-verbal ways such as nodding in agreement, smiling, laughing and showing surprise, being sure that any gesture you make is appropriate.

Putting it all together

You cannot excel in any job over a sustained period of time if you fail to genuinely listen to those who are communicating with you. If others feel that you are not listening, they might think that you are not interested, don't care, are not trustworthy and do not value and respect them. Fortunately, good listening skills are an easily acquired habit which becomes second nature with time. The ability to listen properly makes you come across as someone who has more time for other people and as more selfless than your colleagues.

The three strategies in this chapter are all interconnected – you demonstrate that you are listening by your pauses, by your clarifying questions and, perhaps most importantly, by your entire body language, starting with your eye contact through to not appearing distracted. These are skills that you could teach your team or colleagues. I recently taught a large sales team how to truly listen to their clients and, in the three months that followed my workshops, the company's sales beat budget forecasts by the highest percentage in years!

As you become a better listener, you will increasingly realize that others are not listening to you and you will want to respond to that. Before you jump in to say 'Are you listening to me?' or 'Did you hear what I just said?', try pausing as you speak, repeating key points and then asking those who should be listening 'What do you think of my idea/what I just shared?' They may have difficulty in responding and this may well make them feel embarrassed enough to start listening to the remainder of what you have to say.

29 Ask questions and be inquisitive

> 'He who asks a question is a fool for five minutes; he who does not ask a question remains a fool forever.' Chinese proverb

> 'We run this company [Google] on questions, not answers.'
> Eric Schmidt

> 'Judge a person by their questions, rather than their answers.'
> Voltaire

> 'Asking the right questions takes as much skill as giving the right answers.' Robert Half

> 'The important thing is not to stop questioning. Curiosity has its own reason for existing. Never lose a holy curiosity.' Albert Einstein

If you observe young children, you will notice how many questions they ask; in contrast, when you observe a group of employees in any organization, you will probably notice how little each of them enquires and asks questions of others. We live in a culture where it is sometimes viewed as a weakness to be someone who questions and double-checks things. In meetings, people might be embarrassed to ask a speaker to clarify what they have said or, when being given work instructions by a boss, we might feel uncomfortable double-checking what is being asked of us.

We seem to ask fewer questions and to act as if we know and understand things despite the fact that we are living in a world of increasing complexity where we cannot hope to know everything. A result of not being inquisitive enough is that we make too many assumptions about many of the things we do and this can lead to all kinds of small and large mistakes being made. As a small example, I live in a place that is difficult to find and I warn visitors about this – but so many fail to choose to learn exactly where our house is located until they have been lost for 30 minutes or longer. I joke with them about why they were afraid to call us sooner to ask for more directions.

We must not be lazy and, to excel at work, we must learn to know when to ask questions or seek help, without considering it a weakness. Do not be embarrassed by questions that may come into your mind. Look again at the quotes at the start of this chapter and you will see that they share a common theme – it is better to ask a silly or crazy question than to be seen as silly or crazy for never asking. It is nearly always better to check your understanding of what you are being asked to do than to make mistakes. The secret is in asking the right question of the right person at the right time.

TAKE TIME TO ASK QUESTIONS RATHER THAN TO GIVE ANSWERS

Get into the habit of spending more time asking questions than in giving people answers. In conversations and meetings that you are part of, observe how much time you spend asking questions compared to lecturing and telling others what they should know or do.

There are times when you can learn more and be more effective by simply being inquisitive and asking a question. Even when you think you fully understand what another person is sharing with you and you want to jump in to give a view or an opinion, it is a good idea sometimes to pause and ask a short question, such as: 'Would you welcome my thoughts and opinions?'

I have learned that a good question is better than a good opinion – a question can draw out many opinions and lead to more optimal ideas and outcomes being developed.

Avoid asking questions in a way that suggests that you are not listening to the people you are speaking with. It is good to acknowledge what the other parties are saying before you ask a question. You might say something like:

- 'I hear what you are saying but have you thought about…?'
- 'I see your point but are we also thinking about…?'
- 'I think that you are quite clear but one question that comes to mind is…?'

QUESTION ASSUMPTIONS AND 'TRUTHS'

Do any of the following statements sound familiar from your workplace?

- 'But I thought you meant that.'
- 'But I assumed that you already knew.'
- 'Sorry, I assumed that we would do it the same way as last time.'
- 'Apologies. I never thought to ask because it seemed obvious.'
- 'Why didn't you ask me before you did it?'
- 'Why did you that? I didn't ask you to do it that way.'

We all – although I think that men do this perhaps more than women – have a bad habit of not checking our understanding of things. We all know that, if we are not sure about something, we should ask, but we do not often follow this advice. If you wish to truly succeed, you should be willing to stand out from the crowd by being the one who questions and double-checks things in a way that sounds like you care and want to do the right things. You could make the following kinds of suggestions:

- 'Can I summarize what you are asking us to do?'
- 'May I quickly sum up the agreed plan of action?'
- 'To be sure that we are all in alignment, can I confirm what I understand we should do now?'
- 'To ensure that we get the work done well and to avoid any misunderstandings later, can I email you about what I understand our plan to be?

There are two common mistakes to avoid: don't assume that somebody has already asked the question that you know is important, and don't keep quiet assuming that other people understand something and that they will be able to clarify it with you later. If you did not understand something clearly, there is a high probability that other people did not understand either.

DON'T BE AFRAID TO QUESTION YOUR BOSS AND SENIOR COLLEAGUES

In mid 2012 an airliner crashed when it was coming in to land in San Francisco and investigators found that one key reason for the crash was that a junior pilot had not questioned his more senior colleague. Both pilots were from a country where it is culturally taboo to question elders and, in spite of the plane being in danger of crashing, the younger, more junior pilot was still not comfortable challenging his senior colleague.

This problem is quite common in many workplaces – employees often seem reluctant or sometimes scared to question their boss. Perhaps they fear for their jobs or they fear being told off in public for questioning the person in charge. This is understandable, given that questioning your boss about their decisions and course of action can be seen as challenging and implying that what they are doing is not correct, but you must always have the courage to ask those questions that need asking for the good of the organization. My advice is just to make sure that you do it diplomatically and, if necessary, in private when just the two of you are together.

Putting it all together

Some people's personalities are strong and outgoing and those people may have no hesitation in asking questions when others might be keeping quiet. Such inquisitive people are a minority and the majority of us need to practise speaking up and ensuring that we and our team or colleagues understand what is being communicated and asked of us. We rarely have enough time and resources to do things again if we make mistakes and it only takes a few seconds to clarify and double-check your understanding.

Be seen as the one who asks good questions and listens rather than the one who just has opinions and ideas. You need to be skilled in all these areas and, at times, you need to be assertive by giving your point of view and offering a strong opinion. Avoid the mistake that most people make which is of not being inquisitive and probing but instead simply giving a strong opinion, which can cause others to stop sharing their own ideas with you.

In addition, develop a good habit of double-checking what is being assumed, and learn to ask people diplomatically to clarify what is being asked. Have the confidence and courage to question your boss, whether it is to better understand what they are communicating or to check whether they are doing the right thing.

If you master the strategies described in this chapter, you will find that people want to talk with you and share their ideas with you.

(30) Be assertive and take a stand

❝ *'There's an art to knowing when to speak up and when to back off.'* Layla Kayleigh

❝ *'He who does not have the courage to speak up for his rights cannot earn the respect of others.'* Rene G. Torres

❝ *'Speak only if it improves upon the silence.'* Mahatma Gandhi

❝ *'You have enemies? Good. That means you've stood up for something, sometime in your life.'* Winston Churchill

❝ *'Assertiveness is not what you do, it's who you are!'* Shakti Gawain

There are many times in the workplace when you need to flow with a general consensus. You may not agree with the decisions made and courses of action chosen, but there may be no strong need to oppose them or assert your own views. However, to truly succeed in your career, there will be times when you need to be assertive and take a stand. It might be because you have an insight which others do not have or cannot quickly see, or it might be because you realize that a group is making a clear mistake by taking a particular course of action.

There is always a risk in asserting your opinion and in holding firm when others, including perhaps your boss, have an opposite opinion. But, if you truly believe in what you are standing up for and think it will help your organization, then you must speak up. You will need to use your skills of discernment to weigh up the benefits

137

to the organization and to your career versus any downsides such as upsetting your boss and making yourself unpopular for not supporting the decisions of others. You could face this dilemma in meetings and other group discussions where the majority may not wish to hear or to follow your ideas or arguments.

As well as being assertive about business-related decisions, you may also have to be assertive about your own career needs, including speaking up when you feel that you deserve recognition and opportunities which are not forthcoming.

Being assertive does not mean speaking up loudly in public; often it means raising issues calmly and diplomatically with just your boss or a small group of people. How you proceed will often be influenced by your working environment and culture, and the key is not to become frustrated for having not been assertive enough before. In the 2009 financial crisis, many of the global banks that faced bankruptcy could have avoided financial disaster had more of their staff spoken up earlier and not agreed to go along with the decisions those banks were making in the years leading up to 2009.

DOUBLE-CHECK YOUR FACTS

Before you take a stand, be sure of your foundation in terms of the information, assumptions and arguments that you are basing your position upon. There is nothing worse than stating something quite firmly only for others to undermine you by showing that you did not have all the facts, did not understand something or had made incorrect assumptions. If this were to happen, it might affect your credibility and lead people to question how well you have prepared or researched your points if you wish to assert something important which might conflict with what others think in the future.

If you do not have time to check all the facts but you still wish to make a clear point, you could do so in a way that means you are making a suggestion of something to consider or to explore rather than asserting something which you will stand by 100 per cent. For example, you might say something like: 'I have not had time to double-check all the facts, but shouldn't we consider another option of… because this might be more optimal?'

SEEK ALLIES AND SUPPORTERS

Going it alone can be lonely and leave you exposed. It is better to find like-minded colleagues who are willing to support your argument and to stand firm when others, often the majority, might be pushing in another direction.

Do not blindly believe that others are supporting you until you see tangible signs of support, such as speaking up in meetings or writing supportive emails. Beware of the silent majority who you may think are supporting you when they may actually simply be following whatever their bosses say. Be wary of those who may tell you that they support you but then are saying what a ridiculous point/argument you are making behind your back.

STAND DOWN WHEN NEEDED

Being the one who stood firm and helped the organization to make a correct decision can really help you to stand out and grow your career. However, if you end up as the one who was seen to stubbornly push an idea or point which then turns out to be incorrect or false, things are different.

The secret of your success is to know when to back down and admit that your argument, idea or point may not have been as important or true as you had originally thought. You might have a change of heart because of new information, because of other people's ideas or because you simply realize that what you thought was the optimal solution is not, which often happens when we keep thinking about an issue or problem.

It may be a loss of face for you to be seen to do a U-turn but you must be ready to admit defeat and move on. Great employees are those who are ready to admit when they are wrong – this is a clear sign that a person is growing in wisdom and that their egos are not so large that they are blindly stubborn.

The only time when you might wish to hold firm and stick to what you believe is when it involves issues of conviction, ethics and/or integrity. I know that this is a tricky point – and, indeed, in Chapter 19 I urged you always to do the right thing – but there is a risk that your career with your current organization might suffer. However, bear in mind that you cannot ever claim to be succeeding in the workplace if you find yourself having to sacrifice your integrity just to be liked by your bosses and to gain promotions.

Putting it all together

Some of the world's most successful individuals have been those who had unusual views or ideas in organizations, stood by them and proved with hindsight that those were the best decisions and ideas that could have been made. Standing firm takes courage and self-belief but it can help organizations avoid making potentially costly errors just because the majority have been in support of a decision. Equally, some of the wisest individuals working in organizations know when to stay silent and back off – perhaps they decide to save themselves for a more important challenge or simply realize that their argument is no longer valid.

If you do feel the need to be assertive and to take a stand in a discussion with colleagues, team meeting, management debate or project team, remember the three pieces of advice that I have shared in this chapter. Start by being sure that you are in possession of the facts and that you are on firm ground before you start challenging anyone and taking a stand on an issue. Understand the value of finding allies who will genuinely support you so that you are not a lone voice. And, finally and most importantly, be ready to step back and admit that you were wrong if you realize that your idea, argument or point is not as valuable or critical as you first thought.

(31) Deal with conflict well

❝ *'We should have much peace if we would not busy ourselves with the sayings and doings of others.'* Thomas a' Kempis

❝ *'The Law of Win/Win says, "Let's not do it your way or my way; let's do it the best way."'* Greg Anderson

❝ *'The most difficult thing in any negotiation, almost, is making sure that you strip it of the emotion and deal with the facts.'* Howard Baker

❝ *'If you can't go around it, over it, or through it, you had better negotiate with it.'* Ashleigh Brilliant

❝ *'An apology is the superglue of life. It can repair just about anything.'* Lynn Johnston

Do you work in a company where people argue, fail to communicate well, do not get along, do not trust each other and in which there is always tension in the air? This is more common than you might have imagined and, if you work in such a conflict-filled environment for long, you may even stop noticing it. I like to joke that people become anaesthetized to the pain of the conflicts around them just as we can grow used to a radio playing very loud music in an office.

Conflict in the workplace can be said to occur whenever there are misunderstandings, arguments or disagreements between people. Sometimes the issues and causes are trivial and people quickly forget about them and move on; at the other extreme the causes of conflict can exist for long periods within a team or organization and can cause all kinds of damage to morale and to performance in general.

Think about a recent conflict in your own workplace – what caused it? In my experience, conflict at work can arise for many reasons. The commonest include: personality clashes; poor performance by staff which can create tension; people having different interests, goals, values or motivations; limited resources which different teams or departments might be fighting over; and, finally and very commonly, poor communication.

To be seen as a star performer in your workplace, you need to become a person who never creates conflict and who is able to resolve any conflicts that do occur around you. Act as an arbitrator or referee and, if you become expert at that, you may even be able to foresee issues developing and be able to prevent conflicts from emerging in the first place. Resolving conflict between individuals or groups is never easy and can be harder if you are caught up in the issues personally, but to excel at work you must be ready to do something positive. Doing nothing is not an option. Conflicts are rarely solved by ignoring them and the three strategies below will help you to resolve any conflict that is happening around you and, hopefully, create a harmonious working environment and culture.

REMOVE THE EMOTION FROM EVERYONE'S REACTIONS

People's emotions or their lack of control of their emotions can so often cause small problems to blow up into major conflicts. The secret to stopping such conflicts from emerging or in defusing conflicts once they occur lies in encouraging all those involved to pause before reacting – to calm down, step back and cool down. In soccer you sometimes see players arguing and then other players pulling them apart and telling them to calm down. The equivalent in business would be to intervene in a meeting or discussion when individuals are getting heated and raising their voices. But it's not always easy and it can be particularly hard when you are junior to those arguing, and I would understand if you felt it inappropriate to intervene.

Encourage people to pause before they act and to think about what they are doing. If discussions at work are getting heated, step back and suggest that everyone takes a break.

Emotions can also be an issue when we write to others. Countless misunderstandings are caused by people writing and speaking hastily, perhaps when they are upset about something or jumping to assumptions or conclusions. I offer a simple piece of advice – write your email, memo, fax or letter and then pause before you send it. Type your message, save it and come back to it a few minutes later and ask yourself how you would react if you were to receive that message. Similarly, pause before picking up the phone and leaving a voice message. Do not upset other people or give them cause to complain about you – the worst that could happen is that you lose your job because of one emotion-filled response. Email style and etiquette are explored in more detail in the next chapter.

BE A DETECTIVE – INVESTIGATE AND PROBE

Many conflicts are caused by different people believing, understanding, perceiving or expecting different things; two parties can so easily look at the same situation or information and see two very different pictures. I like to say that facts are friendly and, if the relevant facts about a problem situation can be found and put on the table, it should be possible to resolve any conflict. Finding the facts can take patience and determination and you can sometimes feel like a detective.

Depending on the nature of the conflict, you may need to talk with the various parties directly and indirectly involved and be as objective and balanced as possible, particularly if different people are pushing their own points of view. It can be hard to remain neutral when you might be involved in the problem yourself and may even have a strong point of view. Ideally, you need to step back and take what is called a 'balcony' or 'helicopter' view of the situation. As an example, if you believe that one of your company's departments did or said something wrong and you are tasked with discovering what actually happened, you need to act in a totally unbiased way to explore with colleagues in that department what they did or said and why. You may also need to speak with other people and review any relevant documentation.

Avoid jumping to conclusions by making sure that you listen well to everyone's thoughts and comments and that you read in enough detail whatever paperwork should be reviewed. Let the facts emerge and do not gossip or spread rumours or misinformation.

NEGOTIATE A 'WIN–WIN' SOLUTION SEEKING COMPROMISES

Once the facts have been discovered and shared, there is then a need to sit down and discuss whatever is causing the conflict in order to resolve it. Whether the conflict is between individuals or groups, it is essential to try to find outcomes which leave all parties able to work together afterwards. This can only be achieved if everyone has a 'win–win' mentality and is willing to compromise as needed. This is easier said than done when someone is shown to have been in the wrong and they need to apologize. If you are a guilty party, I encourage you to be humble and apologize, even if you feel you are right and that others only perceive you to be in the wrong. In addition, no parties should ever be allowed to gloat.

Putting it all together

Conflict in the workplace is very common, yet we rarely receive training or coaching in how to resolve it or know how to react when we are caught up in it. It is too easy to become emotional and never gain a full picture.

The three-stage conflict resolution process that has just been described could be called a search for collaborative solutions based on the facts. Solutions are most likely to be found when all parties are calm, emotions have been taken out of the discussions and the relevant facts are known and shared. For this to happen, information cannot be hoarded and hidden and, in my experience, organizations with cultures of openness, trust and sharing suffer less conflict and any conflicts that do arise are resolved more easily than in organizations with closed cultures.

If you really want to excel and to be valued, you must be willing to go further than simply helping to resolve conflicts. You must encourage any parties involved to explore and to learn why the conflict occurred and how and why it was dealt with in the way it was. You need everyone to buy into the idea that the conflict was not needed and was not healthy for the organization. Only through such discussion can you help reduce the chances of similar types of conflict happening again.

32 Work on your email-writing skills

'Either write something worth reading or do something worth writing.' Benjamin Franklin

'You fail only if you stop writing.' Ray Bradbury

'Rudeness is the weak man's imitation of strength.' Eric Hoffer

'Good manners will open doors that the best education cannot.' Clarence Thomas

'To disagree, one doesn't have to be disagreeable.'
Barry M. Goldwater

How many emails do you receive each day? I know people who receive over 1,000, while I also know of some who rarely need to use their company email and only receive a couple of messages in their inbox each week. In the preceding chapter we spoke about how poor communication can be a cause of conflict between colleagues or teams. Poorly planned and written communications can also lead to other problems, including poor work performance, incorrect actions and decisions being taken, opportunities being missed and people being blamed for things unfairly.

Although we sometimes write letters, reports, faxes and memos, the world we live in today is the world of emails. Your company's email system offers a host of benefits: it is easy to access on various devices, has spellchecking features, can automatically save emails as you write them, is able to store emails in sub-folders, enables you to search your email folders and retrieve messages easily… and so the list goes on.

But emails also have a few downsides that you must be aware of. Once you have pressed the 'Send' button, your email has been sent to its recipient(s). Some email systems might give you a short time in which you could stop the sending if you needed to but, as a rule, once you have pressed 'Send', you cannot cancel what you have written. The other downside might sometimes seem to be a benefit – you can create a new email or reply to one that you receive at any time of the day or night – but emails written and sent as you are going to bed can often be regretted in the morning. The final downside is that we are free to write emails of whatever length and in whatever style we choose and we can send them to anyone we wish, and this can cause many problems. The three strategies below will help you overcome these downsides.

PLAN WHAT YOU WISH TO COMMUNICATE AND WITH WHOM

Before you write an email, decide whether email is the ideal medium for communicating your message. Ask yourself whether it would be easier, faster and more effective to speak with the individual on the phone, in person or by video conference. Do not get into a lazy habit of sending an email when you know that you ought to be speaking with the concerned parties in another way.

Some emails are quite easy to write, such as those that are simply confirming things or sharing information. It is emails that cover opinions, proposals and ideas which need extra thought and care because what you say and how you say it can upset people, affect how others view and act towards you and can cause misunderstandings and conflict. Here are some tips for when you are drafting these more sensitive emails:

- Decide the most appropriate time to send the email. It may not be ideal to reply to an important email immediately because this might suggest to the sender that you gave no time and thought to your response.
- Think through what message you wish to communicate in your email. I recently gave coaching to someone

whose boss complained that his emails were always too long and unclear.

- Ensure that the email is neither too long nor too short, and recognize that your organization might have norms on the typical length and form of emails. I have worked with one German company where messages were typically short and to the point, whereas one French client wrote emails that were normally longer than I would choose to write.

- Take care in choosing who you might 'cc' or 'bcc' when you send an email. Are you doing it because you genuinely know that someone needs to be aware of the message and its contents? Be honest with yourself – so many people copy in their bosses in order to show off and be visible, or they might 'cc' someone to protect themselves by showing that they have sent that particular email. If you receive an email with many other recipients copied in, do not feel obliged to click 'reply all' when you reply. Do what you feel is right.

DO NOT REGRET SENDING AN EMAIL

Get the tone and flow of your emails right and try never to send an email when you are tired or angry. You might not agree with someone and you may be upset, but be careful in how you show this in your email. You can show anger to someone face to face when alone and no one else need know exactly how you acted, but emails can so easily be shared with many other people. Avoid writing emails that you will regret having sent. Never be rude in an email communication and never come down to other people's levels of poor or rude communication.

Write your draft email, save it and step back. If you need someone else's opinion, ask a colleague what they think of your draft and whether the wording is appropriate and clearly understandable. Ensure that your messages are culturally sensitive and always ensure that you address people appropriately (using first name or family name, etc.). Once you are happy with your draft email – and only then – you can hit the 'Send' button.

REPLY TO COMMUNICATIONS

Do not be rude by ignoring emails that you are sent. It can be intensely irritating when you send someone an email expecting or needing a reply and you never hear anything. Silence is a form of communication and, if you do not reply to an email, the other party might make assumptions about you – not caring, not being interested, showing no respect, not agreeing with their email's contents, etc.

If you need time to reply to an email, send a holding message stating that you have their email and will reply by a specified time. Show that you value the person's effort in communicating with you and sometimes pick up the phone or go to see the sender of the email if you think it is a more appropriate way of communicating in reply to their email.

As a rule of thumb, if you are 'cc' or 'bcc' on an email, you are not expected to reply and become involved in the discussion, but this often depends on your company's emailing norms and culture as well as the subject of the message.

Putting it all together

We live in a working world in which nearly every one of us sends and receives numerous emails each day and we could not imagine being able to succeed without having easy access to our emails.

We write some of our emails very quickly while others can take a long time to draft and redraft. This chapter is a reminder that how we write our emails has an important impact on how others view and interact with us. You may be like me and have many business contacts who you have never met personally but who you have worked with for many years and communicated through emailing and the occasional phone call. Your emails should reflect your values and personality and this can only happen if you become more thoughtful about when you choose to write an email and how you plan and draft its content. Every email that you send should be an email that you would be happy for anyone to read and that you would never regret having sent. Just as you would expect recipients of your emails to read and to acknowledge them, you must also do the same in return.

In summary, be a colleague who others know will send appropriate and well-written emails and who, in return, will also read and respond to emails that are received. But remember that there are times when no email is needed and you should speak directly – face to face or on the phone – with the other parties.

33 Create excellent meetings

‘Meetings are indispensable when you don't want to do anything.’ John Kenneth Galbraith

‘When you go to meetings or auditions and you fail to prepare, prepare to fail. It is simple but true.’ Paula Abdul

‘People who enjoy meetings should not be in charge of anything.’ Thomas Sowell

‘Our age will be known as the age of committees.’ Ernest Benn

‘Discussion is an exchange of knowledge; an argument an exchange of ignorance.’ Robert Quillen

How many hours do you spend in meetings each week? So many of us spend a large percentage of our working day in meetings with other people – be they colleagues, suppliers, clients and/or other stakeholders. From my experience of coaching so many people, I think that we all spend too much time in meetings and group discussions and we admit that the time spent is not always productive or very useful.

Talking together in different-sized groups is an essential part of how all organizations operate, with meetings necessary to share information and ideas, seek feedback and reach collective agreements and conclusions. I have never met anyone who has a working life which involves no meetings. Even those working remotely or from home may have to attend meetings through Skype, telephone or video conference systems.

151

The alternatives to having face-to-face group meetings can be the sharing of information by emails, teleconferences or collecting information or opinions from each member of a group in one-on-one discussions. Calling people together into a meeting is often seen as the easiest and quickest option for enabling a group to know or agree something. The problems occur when the meeting takes longer than planned or needed and when the topics of discussion wander away from the agreed reason for the meeting. Meetings can also be unproductive when the wrong mix of attendees is present – those who are needed might be absent and those present may not need to be part of the discussions. But perhaps the biggest danger to an organization when people attend meetings is the cost of what they could otherwise be doing with their time – the so-called 'opportunity cost'.

You do not necessarily have to be the organizer or chair of a meeting to be able to influence how that meeting is run to optimize its usefulness. Be aware of the following advice for any meeting that you attend.

DO NOT WASTE PEOPLE'S TIME, INCLUDING YOUR OWN

If you are going to organize a meeting, be clear about why you wish to hold the meeting, who should attend and what the desired outcomes from it are. Decide whether a meeting is the best way of achieving those outcomes. If you simply wish to share information, why not send the group an email or a memo?

If some attendees will have to travel a considerable distance to attend the meeting – for example, for over an hour – why not let them dial in by telephone or video conference? And, if you have to come in a long way yourself, you should ask whether you can attend the meeting 'remotely'. This can work quite well even if you are chairing the meeting.

If it is your meeting, invite only those people who are really needed to enable the meeting to achieve its aims. If you are an invitee and you feel that you do not need to attend a particular meeting, speak up and explain to the meeting's organizer(s) why you think your presence is unnecessary. If they insist on your attendance, ask if you can stay just for the part that is linked to you or (diplomatically) that the meeting starts and finishes on time. In other words, be assertive and show that you value your time.

Know the desired outcomes of meetings that you wish to organize and translate those outcomes into an agenda. If the meeting is needed to discuss topics and make decisions, ensure that all attendees are given sufficient materials to read along with a copy of the agenda prior to the meeting. A good agenda will show the length of the meeting and the length and form of each part of it.

CHAIR DISCUSSIONS WELL

The key advice if you want your team or colleagues to appreciate you chairing a meeting is to follow the agenda and stay on topic. If a meeting is pencilled in for one hour, then it should last for a maximum of one hour. Appreciate that other people, as well as you, have things to do and, even if you are not chairing the meeting yourself, offer to be the meeting's timekeeper and let the chairperson know how much time is being used. People will appreciate this timekeeping.

Being the chair does not mean that you should do all the talking. Instead, listen well and elicit the views and opinions of everyone present. You can then sum up what is being shared, add your thoughts if needed and then help the group to reach consensus and decisions.

Make sure that you determine what follow-up actions are needed, stating who does what and by what dates. If you think that the meeting needs a summary or minutes to be created and circulated after the meeting, you should normally list these agreed follow-up items. Whether you are the chair or an attendee, you could offer to write up the minutes – others will appreciate this and you can always influence what the minutes will actually say.

INVOLVE THE INTROVERTS IN THE MEETING

When you observe a group of people talking together, you will notice that some individuals will speak more than others and might even dominate the content and direction of the discussions. Such people are often those with extrovert personalities who like to verbalize what they are thinking and, if left unchecked, can be the only ones whose opinions are heard.

Introverts are those quieter individuals who feel less need to speak up while they are thinking about something. Although they might appear quiet and less eager to speak up and contribute in meetings, introverts can often provide great insight and ideas because they tend to think about issues and problems for longer than their more outgoing extrovert colleagues might.

In simple terms, extroverts are communicators and introverts are thinkers and a truly productive meeting needs to hear from both groups. So, no matter whether you are chairing a meeting or are simply one of its participants, be ready to seek the contributions of those who are not choosing to speak up. You could simply ask for the thoughts of those who have not spoken on a particular agenda item or you could ask specific people to say what they think.

Putting it all together

Too many people spend too much of their working day in meetings and I often wonder how they have time to do anything else at work. It should come as little surprise that many find their meetings to be too long and not important. I saw a survey which showed that the majority of those who spent time in meetings felt that they were a great time to doodle, answer emails and messages on their smartphones, write to-do lists and think about what they would do as soon as the meeting was over. If you wish to be valued by your colleagues, you must ensure that your meetings are carefully planned with only the necessary participants being asked to attend and the meeting lasting only as long as absolutely necessary.

Once in a meeting, as a chair or participant, ensure that the meeting's discussions and timing stay in line with a well-written agenda. Seek the views and opinions of all attendees, not allowing the extroverts to dominate and the introverts to stay silent. End the different parts of the meeting by summarizing what has been discussed and agreed, including any follow-up needed and stating by whom and by when. This follow-up information should then be written up in meeting minutes, which you should offer to draft.

(34) Learn to accept

> 'We must let go of the life we have planned, so as to accept the one that is waiting for us.' Joseph Campbell

> 'Accept everything about yourself – I mean everything. You are you and that is the beginning and the end – no apologies, no regrets.' Henry Kissinger

> 'The first step toward change is awareness. The second step is acceptance.' Nathaniel Branden

> 'For after all, the best thing one can do when it is raining is let it rain.' Henry Wadsworth Longfellow

> 'Lord, grant me the strength to accept the things I cannot change, the courage to change the things I can, and the wisdom to know the difference.' St Francis of Assisi

Throughout our working lives we face situations, both unexpected and planned, which we may not like or want to have happened in the way they did. It might be a missed promotion opportunity, a major client lost to a competitor, a project which is over budget and taking too long, a great boss who is suddenly fired, a colleague stealing your idea and taking all the credit, or it might simply be that much of your work has become tedious and boring.

To avoid becoming someone who is seen as continually angry, jealous and upset, you must learn to accept and let go of what is happening both to you and around you when you are at work.

But, paradoxically, at the same time I would also encourage you to work on overcoming and solving those same issues that I am saying you must learn to accept. In other words, by asking you to accept what is happening around you, I am not suggesting that you should not push back and try to change those things, but you cannot succeed after a failure if you are full of bitterness, upset, emotion and anger.

Here is an example. If you are a salesman and you fail to secure a customer order which you felt was very important to win, you must not beat yourself up about not having tried hard enough to win that particular client or talk yourself down by complaining and moaning. You need to accept that you are human and that no one can win everything that they want to win. However, there is no reason why you should not try again to win that client or to win equally important new business. Believe that you can succeed if you try again and that this would be a valuable use of your time.

KNOW WHEN TO STOP ARGUING AND FIGHTING

Successful people know when to accept what is happening and they understand that things will not always go the way that they hope, want or feel they deserve. For a time they might challenge and question decisions which have gone against them and sometimes they might even continue the fight when they feel that is the right option but, most of the time, they will learn why they failed to succeed, accept what happened and move on. Once someone has truly made their mind up, you might try to change their view or opinion but you must be ready to stop pushing if it is clear that their decision will not change.

Too many people become quite emotional when work issues do not go the way that they hoped and they seem unable to let go. Perhaps you missed out on being given a grade and job promotion in your company in spite of your feeling that you had done all that you needed to do. In this case, you can react in one of two ways:

- After feeling initially upset and angry, you can accept that not everyone can be promoted and that such processes are not always 100 per cent objective and fair. Once you have accepted what happened, you are in a position to focus on moving forward and trying to be promoted at the next opportunity.
- You might remain upset and angry and start telling people how unfair and biased your bosses are in their promotion decisions. You may write angry emails which you would later regret having sent. You might still be determined to be promoted at the next opportunity but this is unlikely to happen if you hold on to any visible resentment and upset about having just missed out in this round of promotions.

DO NOT ENVY OTHERS

If the promotion example above happened to you, how happy and congratulatory would you be to the colleague who beat you to the promotion? So many people are jealous of their colleagues, neighbours or siblings. Too easily we envy what they have achieved without understanding the price that they might have paid. Watching your colleagues achieve more work-related success and recognition than you are achieving may not be easy, particularly if you feel that you should have been given or obtained what they have.

We have to learn to accept that the world is unequal and that, just as you are more successful in your work than others, there will always be someone who could be seen as being more successful than you. To truly excel at work you must be seen as a colleague and leader who does not envy or feel jealous of others around you. People should not have to think twice about sharing their success stories with you. Practise feeling and showing that you are happy for all of your colleagues' successes – be they business deals, promotions, work well done or whatever – even when they may succeed at your expense.

LEARN TO GO WITH THE FLOW

Take to heart the quote at the start of this chapter from St Francis of Assisi: know that there are things that you cannot change and that, throughout your working life, such things will be thrown across your path for you to challenge or accept.

Know that, when one door of opportunity closes, another one might well open up. You may miss a promotion today but others will come along. I urge you to learn to expect the unexpected and to look back at your working career to date to be reminded that not everything went to plan but that things have worked out.

Putting it all together

You can never truly succeed in your work and career if you hold on to things from the past that did not go as planned and also if you are jealous of other people. So much workplace stress and unhappiness comes from people being angry and upset about what is happening around them and being unwilling to accept that some things have simply happened and we must move on. In some Asian cultures there is a more natural tendency to accept, but in Europe and North America we are more individualistic and seem to be less willing to accept when things do not go as we planned or hoped and we too easily envy our more successful work colleagues.

It is not hard to stand out in a positive way wherever you are working by being the one who is not continually complaining and moaning about things not going your way; be the one who is genuinely happy for the success enjoyed by your colleagues; and, finally, be the colleague who is able to go with the flow, telling others not to worry if an opportunity is missed and that there are many more 'fish in the sea to be caught'. If you can be like this, you can have a working life of fewer regrets and in which you are not continually looking back to the past at what you see as all your mistakes and missed opportunities. This will leave you with more time to focus on working well today as well as having more time to plan for your future work and career.

35 Manage your time well

Do you have enough time to complete everything that you need to do at work this week? How many hours do you spend working each day? Include all the time you work, including those few minutes that you might spend reading company emails on your phone when you are going to bed.

I rarely meet a person who claims that they have enough hours in the working day to be able to give enough time to all of their tasks and complete everything well. We all seem to have unread emails, reports not completed and important conversations that have been delayed and most of us are handling too many things and are struggling to multitask well.

We are limited to 24 hours in a day and we need to make best use of our day to enable us to excel in our work. Staying in our workstations or offices until late at night on a regular basis is not sustainable and does not offer an acceptable work–life balance. If this is the price required of you in order to complete all of your work really well, I would say that either how you do your work has to change or you need to consider changing your work.

It is safe to say that very few people can do everything that is asked of them in the time frames that others might expect, and the secret to success is to choose wisely what tasks we take on and to plan how we complete the work. You need to decide whether you will spend time doing just one task or whether you will multitask by doing a few things at the same time. You must also decide when to accept work tasks, when to delegate work and when you might push back and reject requests for your help, weighing up the pros and cons of potentially upsetting the person asking you to do something.

DECIDE WHAT IS URGENT AND WHAT IS IMPORTANT

Start by regularly making 'to-do' lists, writing them at the end or at the start of each week or month. It doesn't matter where you put them – type them into your smartphone or handwrite them in a notebook – or how you maintain them, but be sure to make them. Decide how important and how urgent each item on the list is and try to map out when you plan to do each task. I always like to start by completing the quick and easy tasks, the so called 'low-hanging fruit', to make the remaining list appear shorter and more manageable.

An important area requiring good time management is dealing with your emails, particularly if you receive hundreds each day and even where sometimes you are only 'cc' or 'bcc'. Try to get into a good habit of working out which of your emails you have to read in detail, which you can skim read and which you can ignore. Many people like to create sub-folders for their emails, including folders for emails that still need to be replied to and those that need to be acted on in some way.

DELEGATE WHEN YOU CAN

Once you have created a 'to-do' list and have determined the levels of importance and urgency of all of your pending tasks and email requests, you should then make a decision about whether you will complete the task yourself or delegate some or all of the work. Delegating work is a learned skill and is not easy to do well because you are requesting and imposing on other people over whom sometimes you may have no formal authority; you cannot therefore simply order them to do something for you.

Decide whether an entire task needs delegating to someone else or whether it would be more efficient to ask someone to do part of it for you, perhaps gathering some data, checking an Excel spreadsheet or finding a report for you.

There may be times when you will need to ask your boss to do something for you to ease your workload. This may not be an easy request, particularly when it might have been your boss who gave you that particular task in the first place. Such so-called 'upward delegation' takes diplomacy and tact and, most importantly, it needs an understanding and caring boss.

Are you the sort of person who finds it hard to let go and to trust others? Do you prefer to do a task yourself, even if it might be wiser to ask someone else to do it for you? Some people are not used to sharing the burden of their work and will always find excuses to justify that, the commonest ones being that it is easier and faster to do it themselves and they can be sure of the work's quality.

LEAVE THE WORKPLACE ON TIME

Some of the busiest and most productive people I know always try to leave work on time and not to spend any longer than needed in the office. This is partly because of their after-work commitments but it also reflects their desire to use the working day as productively as possible and to work as smartly as possible to ensure that they finish all that they need to do during normal working hours.

You might respond that there are times when you really need to stay at work longer to complete some urgent work. That may be the case, but make those days the exception and not the norm. Ideally, leave work on time at least three out of five times in the week.

I do hope that you do not have a boss or senior colleague who sees you leaving the office on time and makes comments such as, 'Leaving already?' or 'Have you no work to do?' If you do, I would encourage you to be strong: be polite but leave the office when you planned to. Never feel compelled to stay at work unless you genuinely feel that you have to; pleasing your boss should never be a sole reason to stay late at work.

Putting it all together

The lack of time is often the main hurdle facing all of us, no matter where and how we work. The modern business world has become one of constant deadlines, being late and rushing to do things. It is not easy to manage your time well, particularly when others, including your bosses, might want a big say in how you use your time. How often have you been asked something along the lines of 'Could you help me to do this now it is urgent – it will only take you about 20 minutes maximum?' And an hour or two later you are still toiling on this '20-minute' task, having dropped your other urgent tasks which will still need doing today before you are able to go home.

Have the courage to set boundaries on how you spend your day: try to take ownership of your own to-do list, clearly showing the order in which you plan to complete tasks depending on your definitions of urgency and importance. If you are challenged by someone as to why you have not completed something for them, walk them through your list. The danger is that you will put their work at the top of the list every time someone complains – rather like piling sand on top of a sandcastle.

163

36 Be creative and innovative

> **"** 'Curiosity about life in all of its aspects, I think, is still the secret of great creative people.' Leo Burnett

> **"** 'You can't wait for inspiration. You have to go after it with a club.' Jack London

> **"** 'Creativity is just connecting things. When you ask creative people how they did something, they feel a little guilty because they didn't really do it, they just saw something. It seemed obvious to them after a while.' Steve Jobs

> **"** 'You see things; and you say, "Why?" But I dream things that never were; and I say, "Why not?"' George Bernard Shaw

> **"** 'Creativity is contagious. Pass it on.' Albert Einstein

How creative and innovative are you? Think of the last time you shared with your boss or colleagues a new idea or concept – was it yesterday, last week or last year?

Being creative and innovative is all about seeking better, newer and more productive ways of doing things. It is about seeing new things and imagining new possibilities in ways that others may miss or have not thought of before. It is possible for anyone in any job or profession to use their creativity and innovation and it is not only confined to creative jobs – being creative and innovative is a mindset which comes from experience and from being inquisitive, open-minded and taking the initiative.

Creative and innovative ideas and solutions can be found in all areas of any business or organization and within any job function. These new ideas might relate to seemingly small matters, such as how data is entered into a system by a clerk or how to change some Excel spreadsheet equations to make the spreadsheet easier to understand, through to large solutions, such as how an organization rebrands itself or how it introduces a new product.

Organizations grow and thrive primarily because of a healthy culture of creativity and innovation, enabling products and solutions, and all the internal processes, to be refined, developed and grown to meet changing client and stakeholder needs and expectations. As a result, you cannot continually succeed and hope to be promoted if you are not being creative and innovative in your role.

ASK QUESTIONS AND ENCOURAGE BRAINSTORMING

As you do your work, try to be open to finding new and better ways of doing things and also try to find innovative solutions to any problems and challenges that you face. If you would like to be able to do your work in more efficient and effective ways, then you must be ready to try new ideas and take heed of the quote attributed to Rita Mae Brown:

'Insanity is doing the same thing over and over again but expecting different results.'

The easiest way to find new solutions and ideas is to question the status quo by asking yourself and others probing questions such as these:

- How might we complete this task faster next time?
- Is all this information really required by the team every month?
- How might we reduce the product development lead-time?
- Let's explore how we can simplify this process.
- Why does it take so long to take customer feedback? Is there no faster way?

Try asking a question like this that you think needs discussing and bring a team or group together to brainstorm, ideally with a flipchart, to capture ideas coming from and solutions to the question.

START CAPTURING YOUR IDEAS 24/7

This might sound like a crazy suggestion but I encourage you to capture ideas and thoughts that come to you. Something interesting might occur to you in a meeting, in the shower or while you are driving to work. You might see new threads and links between what someone is telling you and other tasks that you are working on. Keep problems in your mind and allow ideas to come to you. I know someone who frequently goes to bed thinking about a problem and often wakes up in the middle of the night with a flash of inspiration.

A couple of great and simple tools to help you capture your ideas are mind maps (also called spider diagrams) and doodles. They are a way of making notes in the form of connected ideas and points, and can help you see things in fresh ways. Type 'mind maps' into Google images to see some examples. The next time you need to make a to-do list, try drawing it in the form of a mind map. You might think of doodling as simply sketching nonsense but actually, when you are thinking of problems that need solving or you are looking for new ideas, having a pen and paper can enable you to capture ideas and thoughts in whatever form comes to mind.

Find your own way of capturing your thoughts – I had a colleague who used to carry an mp3 recorder and he would dictate his ideas and write them down later. But a word of warning: if ideas tend to come to you in the shower, make sure your recorder is waterproof!

ACT YOUNG: BE READY TO LET GO OF THE 'OLD' TO LET IN THE 'NEW'

You might recall Chapter 18's advice about accepting and embracing change, and it should not surprise you to hear that a person who is not open to change might have a problem being innovative and creative. Younger people are more capable of accepting change as well as thinking of new solutions, ideas and ways of doing things. This is partly because a younger person has fewer established ideas and ways of doing things in their heads, whereas an older person has entrenched ideas and habits which they may have to dispose of when they embrace something new.

My advice to all of you is to act younger than your age and get into the habit of letting go of any ideas and habits which you realize have been superseded by more innovative and creative solutions. Be ready to experiment and to try out new ideas at work and show your boss and colleagues that you are willing to take the risk of and invest the time in implementing new solutions and processes. In meetings and discussions, be the one who says: 'I am happy to try out this new idea with my team' or 'I am happy to trial this new process to see how it can help my department.'

Putting it all together

We live in an increasingly complex working world where there is constant pressure to do new things and to create new ideas. You cannot stand out and excel in any line of work unless you are willing to be creative and innovative on a daily basis. This means that you must encourage yourself to be open-minded and to question what you see and experience. You can learn to behave like this even if you are convinced that you are not a very creative person.

Start being seen by your colleagues as the person who has ideas and who seeks new and better ways of doing things. Help other people with their problems by looking for new and innovative solutions through having productive brainstorming sessions. Be ready to question how tasks could be carried out faster, more cheaply and more effectively.

Get into the habit of capturing your ideas and moments of inspiration – those eureka moments. You may like to try making mind maps and doodling, doing whatever works for you to ensure that, as you reflect over questions and problems, you can be sure of recording your ideas.

And, finally, remember to stay young and receptive to new things and new ideas. Encourage your colleagues to be 'young at heart' too, and together challenge yourselves to work and think in crazy, creative and innovative ways.

(37) Be a skilled decision-maker

'Choices are the hinges of destiny.' Pythagoras

'A problem clearly stated is a problem half solved.'
Dorothea Brande

'To get anywhere, or even to live a long time, a man has to guess, and guess right, over and over again, without enough data for a logical answer.' Robert Heinlein

'The quality of decision is like the well-timed swoop of a falcon which enables it to strike and destroy its victim.' Sun Tzu

'Once you make a decision, the universe conspires to make it happen.' Ralph Waldo Emerson

What do you do at work which does not involve making a decision? Virtually everything we do involves having to decide something – where to sit in a meeting, what to say to your boss, when to call a client, what to wear to a presentation, what to drink at coffee break, how to write an important email… The list is endless and just about the only things that do not require a decision are those things that you have learned to do and can do without thinking, those tasks that you can do 'with your eyes closed' on autopilot. Indeed, I was once on a course which shared the idea that our entire lives are simply a connection of millions of decisions, both small and large, and that success can be strongly correlated to how well you are able to make and to influence all the decisions which impact upon you.

There is no way that you could hope to excel at work without being an excellent decision-maker and knowing when you are able to make a decision alone and when you need the help and advice of others. This is an important example of using your discernment, which we explored in Chapter 25.

Great chess players are able to think about their future possible moves following any move that they may be planning to make now. Good decision-making is like playing chess and you must avoid making hasty decisions without thinking of how that particular decision will impact on different aspects of your work and organization. The worst kind of decision-making is deciding to delay a difficult decision until later or to pass it to someone else to have to make. You will never excel and be valued by your colleagues if you get into these habits of procrastination and passing responsibility to others.

DO NOT SHORTCUT THE PROCESS WHEN MAKING IMPORTANT DECISIONS

Decision-making is a process involving two key variables – information and solutions.

- Some decisions can be made with limited information while others need far more data and information to enable an informed decision to be made.
- Some decisions can be reached only after considering many possible options or outcomes; in other cases there may be only one or two possible options.

Some decisions at work can be made quickly with very little thinking and analysis, but you must not make the mistake of failing to recognize when a decision that you are trying to make requires you to evaluate a large amount of information and has many potential outcomes. Do not try to shortcut this process by looking at only some of the information and possible outcomes. If you do, then do not be surprised when your chosen decision turns out to have been the wrong choice.

Observe how you normally make decisions. Do you skim read information and then jump to one possible conclusion or outcome which seems the obvious choice? Or do you like to take your time, digesting all the information available and calmly weighing up the possible options. We all get into decision-making habits and I encourage you to learn when to use your normal style and when you might:

- be more decisive than normal and quickly arrive at a chosen solution
- need to delay making a decision while you spend time gathering more feedback or information.

Good decision-making requires good judgement and discernment, skills which you explored in Chapter 25.

CHALLENGE OTHER PEOPLE'S DECISIONS, INCLUDING THOSE OF YOUR BOSS

Have you experienced an occasion when your boss or another senior colleague made a decision about something that was important and which you felt was not the right decision or was a decision which you could not understand? If something like this happens, try never simply to accept the decision without at least trying to understand why it was made. Keeping quiet might allow you to avoid having to challenge those more senior than you but, if you feel that a particular decision needs to be reviewed, questioned or simply explained and understood better, then speak up by diplomatically asking:

- Have we made the right decision?
- Was this really the optimal choice?
- Could you explain why you made the decision that you did?
- How well did we explore other options?

Have the courage to share the reasoning that leads you to think that a decision that has been taken may not have been the ideal one. Often that will not be easy and I do understand that in some cultures, such as in North Asia, it is not acceptable to question and to challenge a senior colleague as freely as one might do in Europe or in North America.

FACILITATE EXCELLENT GROUP DECISION-MAKING DISCUSSIONS

When working in a group or team, the optimal decision-making process is one that involves everybody and where decisions are reached by consensus, collaboration and compromise. It is important that you encourage group members to listen to all the views and opinions, particularly those of the quieter introverts who are often more thoughtful than others and may offer some important insights.

When you are the leader or chairperson of group discussions, you may have to make some difficult choices, such as bringing opposing points of view together, imposing a corporate viewpoint or cutting off discussion in the interests of time. At the same time, you should ensure that you recognize everybody's opinions and decide quite openly how a collective decision will be reached, the most common process being to call for a vote through a show of hands. Your most difficult role will be to help all those who supported an alternative outcome to come on board and support the final decision and this will involve you spending time talking with those individuals.

Putting it all together

I know that you can make excellent decisions – after all, you have chosen to read this book and have reached this chapter! Indeed, most people – through a combination of prior experience, copying others and learning from their mistakes – become reasonably good at making decisions in their areas of work, but being quite good at decision-making is not enough to ensure that you stand out and excel in your work and career. You need to aspire to be excellent in the decisions that you make and in how you contribute to a group or team's decision-making process.

Being aware of how you make decisions is key, as is trying to make sure that each decision-making process that you are part of is optimal. You can ensure this only by making a final decision once you have reviewed enough information and after considering enough possible outcomes. Realize that sometimes you can make a wise decision in ten seconds but in other cases it might take you a few days to be able to arrive at a final conclusion. Do not rush decisions, even when you think the solution is obvious – at least pause and reflect for a few moments to be sure that you are making the wisest choice.

Have the courage to question other people's decisions, even those of your boss, when you think that they may be making the wrong choices. When you are involved in group decisions, be the person who leads your colleagues to the best decisions possible.

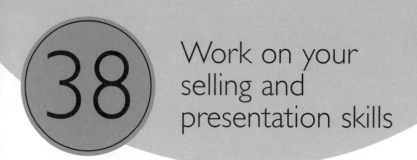

38 Work on your selling and presentation skills

'No one can remember more than three points.' Philip Crosby

'Understand that you need to sell you and your ideas in order to advance your career, gain more respect, and increase your success, influence and income.' Jay Abraham

'Some people fold after making one timid request. They quit too soon. Keep asking until you find the answers. In sales there are usually four or five "no's" before you get a "yes".' Jack Canfield

'No one ever complains about a speech being too short!' Ira Hayes

'We love to hear stories. We don't need another lecture. Just ask your kids.' Unknown

Are you someone who enjoys standing up and speaking or do you suffer from stage fright? When presenting to colleagues or clients, do you get quite nervous or do you find it fun and relaxing? Most people get nervous and anxious when they have to present something, feeling exposed and fearing that others will be critical of what and how they are communicating. Although it is difficult for some, we all need to master how we sell and present because we must present and sell things all the time during a typical working day – opinions, proposals, ideas and arguments. Sometimes the presentation is formal, with us standing on a podium, but most often we are presenting in all kinds of informal or impromptu settings and situations.

Think of people who present well. What is it that you admire or like about how they present and sell their ideas? Is it their body language, tone of voice, choice of phrases, flow of their arguments? Studies of impactful speakers and people selling things show that the most successful are those who are able to make an emotional connection with their audience in addition to making an intellectual or mental connection. In other words, good presenters are able to make you understand why something is good while also making you feel that you want to have or to accept what they are presenting.

When trying to win over other people – be it a small group of colleagues, an individual client or a lecture room full of people – understand that what you actually say is only a part of how you can influence them. In addition, you must understand that other things can be equally if not more important, including your mood and emotions, the clothes you wear, how you stand and move as you speak, your eye contact with your audience, and how you pause, reflect and ask questions.

PRACTISE 'IN THE MIRROR' AND BELIEVE IN WHAT YOU SEE

Very few people can present well without preparation, even when giving those so-called 'off the cuff' speeches or presentations.

Many people do not like the sound of their own voice or do not enjoy watching themselves present in the mirror. Learn to accept how you sound and how you look when presenting, committing to improve yourself if need be but without critically beating yourself up about how you sound and look. This involves you viewing yourself positively as someone who can present well, who is worth listening to and who deserves to be taken seriously.

Remember a small truth that I have learned after many years of coaching people – nobody is ever truly ready and fully an expert in what they are selling or presenting. But, if we practise, we can come across as being quite fluent and expert in our fields. Our requests, arguments or whatever else we are presenting can come across to any audience quite convincingly.

Always try to emulate great presenters. Consider asking an experienced colleague who presents well to listen to you practising your presentation and ask them for their constructive feedback on your performance. Ask them to comment on what you said, how you looked and the quality of any materials used, such as PowerPoint slides. Perhaps such a person could mentor and coach you to becoming a more polished presenter by giving you a few lessons, spending an hour every couple of weeks working on your selling and presentation skills?

When presenting – be it seated in your office or standing around a conference table – practise good body language, remembering what you learned from Chapter 26: do not move too much, look happy, smile and look your audience in the eye without staring at them.

GIVE GOOD 'ELEVATOR SALES PITCHES'

By 'elevator sales pitch' I mean being able to give short, succinct and to-the-point presentations where you remember to KISS (short for 'keep it simple, stupid'). In our working world of information overload and 24/7 communications, understand that less is better than more. Brevity rather than length should be evident in all aspects of your presentation, such as in the length of speech, having fewer slides than you might have first planned, keeping sentences and arguments short, and aiming to make just a few points. In addition, always leave pauses and moments of silence and listen well to your audience.

Phil Crosby's quote at the start of this chapter is very true but, if you must exceed three points, try never to exceed seven unless you are happy to lose an audience and leave them unable to remember what it is that you wanted them to hear. So many times I hear a conversation such as: 'What was he trying to say in his presentation?' and someone replies, 'I'm actually not sure.'

Aim to give a memorable presentation in which you are able to summarize your ideas, requests and points into a few seconds or at most a couple of minutes. Repeat your key points to help reinforce them, recognizing that people have short attention spans. Even if you need to give a long presentation that might last an hour or more, test yourself by being able to verbally summarize what you wish to communicate in a short three-minute presentation.

FOLLOW UP WELL

You need to avoid people saying the following kinds of things after you have presented to them:

- 'I like her idea but she never came back as promised with a more detailed presentation.'
- 'His presentation and arguments are great, but where is the summary email he was asked to send us all after the meeting?'

After you have made your presentation or sales pitch, agree with your audience the next steps and who will do what. Listen well to what your audience thinks and says they want. Do you need to offer to meet again to clarify any points? Do you need to send a follow-up email with some additional information or a simple summary of what you have presented or requested? Put yourself in your audience's shoes and ask yourself what more they might need to know or do in order to be able to support what you were asking of them.

Only through experience, practice and repetition can we become expert in presenting and selling our ideas, proposals, arguments or products to other people. Never step unprepared into a meeting where you must present something – practise beforehand what you wish to say, being clear about who your audience is and what exactly they need to hear to ensure that your message is communicated and understood clearly. Remember what we discussed in Chapter 28 – you need to listen well to ensure that you understand what your audience is thinking and feeling during and after your presentation. Just because you think that you presented well does not mean that your audience is going to agree and buy into whatever it is that you are asking of them.

To truly excel in a role which requires you to present often, you do need to be comfortable presenting; otherwise you may struggle to perform well in your job. Some people are extroverts and are happy standing up and sharing; for others it can be quite daunting. Perhaps you are someone with an introvert personality? If you find it very hard and uncomfortable to present to others, you might be advised to try growing your career by only taking on job roles where you are not required to present to others very often, instead focusing on jobs where the tasks are more aligned with your areas of strength and interest.

39 Work well with your colleagues in teams

66 *'No man is wise enough by himself.'* Plautus

66 *'Coming together is a beginning. Keeping together is progress. Working together is success.'* Henry Ford

66 *'We must all hang together, or assuredly, we shall all hang separately.'* Benjamin Franklin

66 *'Talent wins games, but teamwork and intelligence win championships.'* Michael Jordan

66 *'It is amazing how much people get done if they do not worry about who gets the credit.'* Swahili proverb

If I were to ask your colleagues what you are like to work with as a member of the same team or group, what would they say about you? Are you a great team player? Hopefully, after you have read and implemented this book's secrets and techniques, you will be viewed as a perfect model colleague whom everyone would love to work alongside!

During their working careers, most people will be a member of many different teams, departments and groups within their workplaces. This chapter offers important advice for when you are simply a member of a team and are not leading it, whether it is a senior management team or a team of salesmen or engineers. Advice for when you are leading and managing teams is given in Chapter 41.

No matter how successful you are as an individual employee, you need to able to work well in teams. Sometimes these are virtual or remote teams requiring different skills and particularly good communications skills but it is extremely rare to meet someone who can claim to work totally alone and never need to be part of any teams at all.

A group or team of colleagues is essentially a collection of different personalities, communication styles and mindsets. Even when two colleagues may have identical jobs and very similar-looking work experience, they can be quite different people to work with – for instance, one might have a very aggressive and selfish personality while the other might be extremely collaborative and consensus-seeking. It is because of each person's uniqueness that teams can have all kinds of difficulties as well as remarkable successes.

BE SOMEONE WHOM OTHERS LIKE TO WORK WITH

You cannot excel in your work on a daily basis if you do not get on with people with whom you work or if you are not a person others like to work with. Sandra Day O'Connor, the first female US Supreme Court justice, once gave some great advice that sums up well what it takes to truly get along with work colleagues:

> 'Treat people well. Don't mislead them. Don't be prickly.'

Aim to be someone whom colleagues will naturally turn to for help and support, someone with whom they wish to work, whom they trust and are happy to collaborate with. This can be achieved in a number of seemingly simple ways:

- Start by being pleasant and kind. Cultivate this so that it comes naturally and will develop into a daily habit. If you are upset with a colleague, pause before reacting to ensure that what you communicate is not too emotional or angry.
- Be honest with your colleagues, avoiding saying one thing in front of them and something different behind their backs. Only say things to your colleagues that

you would not mind them saying to you. Do not play games, for example by withholding information from your colleagues. Being honest and open will enable your colleagues to learn to trust you, without which I do not believe that two people can ever optimally work and succeed together.

- Try never to appear selfish, even when you know that you might be acting in a way to benefit yourself. Give your colleagues credit when they have contributed to something which you have done well.
- Give time to developing good working relationships with your colleagues. Get to know new colleagues through socializing, perhaps having lunch with them.
- Be generous and helpful – this very important behaviour is expanded upon below.

These pieces of advice sound very easy, but they are not easy for us to perform day in, day out. Too often, people forget to share or to be honest – perhaps out of fear that a colleague will be offered a promotion instead of them or because they have a selfish moment and want to be the only one who impresses a boss. Yes, you do need to look after your own career success and, yes, you might achieve short-term success by acting selfishly and dishonestly with your colleagues. But such behaviour cannot give you lasting long-term success – your colleagues will remember how you treated them and, as they or you are promoted, you may find that they will not wish to work with you. You may even find yourself losing your job as result.

LEARN INSTINCTIVELY TO LIKE YOUR COLLEAGUES

How many of your colleagues do you not particularly like or not get on with in some way?

I often hear people in organizations making comments such as:

- 'I do not think she likes me.'
- 'He never seems to talk with me.'
- 'Not sure what I did wrong but he never involves me in the discussions.'

People often think that a colleague does not like or get on with them. If left unchecked, such thoughts can become reality because a person who thinks they are disliked might start to avoid connecting with the other colleague and may even start thinking badly of them. From my coaching work I know that perceptions like these are often wrong and the other colleague does not have any negative feelings towards the colleague who is mistakenly thinking otherwise.

As a result, it is not enough to think that you like and get on well with all of your colleagues; you need to ensure that they know you like and get on with them. The best way of letting someone know that you value, like and enjoy having them as a colleague is to tell them and to show them through how you treat them – involve them, share with them and help them.

HELP YOUR COLLEAGUES WHEN THEY ARE IN NEED

How often do you help your colleagues? Only when they actively seek out your advice or as soon as you see them struggling? Understand that you cannot base a career on succeeding only because you do not stumble or fail, while those around you might.

We all struggle at some point with our work, particularly if our roles and tasks change. When a colleague is struggling with a particular task or issue, you have a choice – either you leave them with their struggle or you step in to help them. Do the latter every time – be the first colleague to offer to help, to coach and to mentor your colleagues.

Putting it all together

Developing great working relationships with colleagues might sound like an obvious and simple strategy for success. It might be both obvious and simple but, because of people's perceptions, emotions and interpersonal skills, it is common for colleagues not to get on well and for there to be a lack of trust, sharing and communication. This problem can be heightened when colleagues come from different cultures or are located in other offices.

Start by being someone whom your colleagues would call a great member of the team, someone they enjoy working with and with whom they are happy to share and interact on a daily basis. If you can achieve this, then you have created a great platform from which you can excel in your work. In return, you are encouraged always to learn to like and get on with all your colleagues. This might entail you overlooking those moments when a colleague might not have given you due credit or might have withheld information. Do talk about such incidents with your colleagues but then move on in a positive way. Show your colleagues that you appreciate and value them – this can be as simple as a thank-you email through to telling your boss how helpful someone has been on a project that you have just completed.

Finally, to maintain a great relationship with your colleagues, always be ready to help, offering your time and support when they are needed. This will help you create what is called a 'positive emotional bank balance' and, when you need your colleagues' help, they will be much more likely to reciprocate happily.

40 Work well with your boss

'If you think your teacher is tough, wait until you get a boss. He doesn't have tenure.' Bill Gates

'If you think your boss is stupid, remember: you wouldn't have a job if he was any smarter.' John Gotti

'Show me a man who is a good loser and I'll show you a man who is playing golf with his boss.' Jim Murray

'No man goes before his time, unless the boss leaves early.' Groucho Marx

'Accomplishing the impossible means only the boss will add it to your regular duties.' Doug Larson

Bosses are key individuals in our work and career lives – they are the ones who are normally most influential in grading us, training us, motivating us and, we hope, promoting us into more senior roles. The extent to which we get on with our own boss can play a large part in how successful we will be: a boss with poor skills of motivation and communication might not bring out the best in one person but another employee might flourish under the same boss.

Many people find it hard working with their boss and often leave their jobs because of their boss's working style, behaviours and attitude. I once heard someone say, 'I joined the company, but I left my boss.' I too have left jobs because I felt unable to work under my boss any longer but, with hindsight, I know that if someone had offered me advice on how to work well with a boss, I might have been able to continue working in those jobs.

I cannot imagine anyone being able to succeed in their work and career if they do not get on well with their boss. It is an essential skill but it can be a hard one to learn when you do not like or respect that person. Many of the techniques in this book, when mastered, will naturally help you to get on well with anybody with whom you work, including your boss. But getting on well with a boss requires a few extra skills – showing them respect, particularly when with other people, learning from them, sharing with them and being open and honest. It also involves knowing when to delegate to the boss and when to offer to help and, perhaps most importantly, giving your boss credit and recognition and help to shine.

ENABLE YOUR BOSS TO SHINE AND SUCCEED

Giving your boss as much credit and visibility as possible should benefit both of you. Your boss is likely to appreciate you making such an effort and will value you as a member of his team. In certain cultures, in Asia for example, one always gives the boss recognition or what is called 'face' – even when the staff may have done the really good work, it is often one's boss who takes the accolades. You could adapt this idea when you have completed some work well, by acknowledging the support and help of your boss as well as of any colleagues or team members who helped you.

Giving your boss recognition is hard for some people to do, particularly where there are issues of trust and where a boss never gives their staff any credit or recognition. In such cases it is understandable that you might be reluctant to give your boss any kind of recognition or support. But, if this is the situation, then I suggest that you force yourself, hoping that it will encourage them to become more generous.

You can also help your boss to succeed by sharing any information or gossip that you hear that could impact on your boss and the team. This is particularly helpful when you know something earlier than others and, by telling your boss, you are giving them valuable time to prepare and to react. I would call this a positive example of office politics.

You must remember your own need to shine and there will be moments when you wish to give yourself, and not others, including your boss, the visible credit for a job well done. In such cases it might be normal in your organization to write an email to a wide group of people sharing news about the completed project or deal closed. But would it not be even more impactful if you were to ask your boss to write and to send such an email in which they acknowledge you? In this way you are showing that you value the boss's input and role.

KNOW WHEN TO TAKE WORKLOAD OFF YOUR BOSS'S SHOULDERS

We are all very busy and it might sound foolish to suggest that we must ask our boss for extra tasks to increase our workload. It is a question of offering at key moments when you can see that your boss has a number of critical tasks to do and you feel comfortable that you could undertake some of them. Be conscious of how these extra tasks might increase your own workload; I would caution you from offering to take on work if it will entail long hours of overtime, stress and a lack of work–life balance. The secret is to offer to help your boss when you know you have time.

You might offer to do something which will also give you some extra visibility, for instance with your boss's boss or with other departments. You might also take on a task which will enable your boss to see you in a new light, perhaps completing something that he or she may not have thought you capable of.

Your colleagues might be envious of you and may even gossip that you are trying to be in your boss's 'good books' by being so willing to take on extra work. Your colleagues would be correct but people who excel in their workplace will always have colleagues who will make negative comments and you may need to develop a thicker skin and accept critical comments being made.

BECOME YOUR BOSS'S OBVIOUS SUCCESSOR

This builds on the previous two strategies which, if carried out well, ought to make you a strong contender to be your boss's successor or someone whom your boss supports for promotions, either within the team or elsewhere in the organization. The secret is to become the person within your boss's team who stands out and is the person that your boss would instinctively turn to when there is a question or idea to bounce off someone. To achieve this, you must first master the two previous strategies – giving your boss credit and helping him or her to shine while also offering to relieve some of the workload.

You must also ensure that you are up to date and expert in the range of skills, knowledge and behaviours that are needed to be able to do your boss's job. The advice in Chapter 27 on becoming an avid learner will help you to undertake whatever learning is required.

Putting it all together

For the work and career success of nearly all of us, the most important and influential person is our current boss or, in the increasingly common world of dual or matrix reporting lines, our bosses. Your boss is your most important colleague and you need to invest time in optimizing your relationship with him or her. Much of the advice in this book should be used when interacting with your boss so that they can see that you possess and use a full range of skills appropriately, which will help both of you to succeed. This chapter has given you three distinct strategies to help you to truly stand out and become your boss's right-hand man or woman.

Helping your boss to be successful and viewed in a positive light is not easy because we are so used to wanting the spotlight and credit to focus on us. But how can you hope to excel in your career if your boss is not seeing you as being really supportive and helpful of his or her own career?

Be thoughtful in helping reduce your boss's workload by offering to take on tasks that you feel confident of being able to do well and that, by completing, will mean you are seen in a positive light by your boss and other colleagues.

Although you may not aspire to be your boss's successor, being viewed as the successor has to be the highest accolade that can be bestowed upon someone who is having a very positive relationship with their boss.

41

Work well with your own staff

> 'Catch someone doing something right.' Kenneth Blanchard and Spencer Johnson

> 'Hire people who are better than you are, then leave them to get on with it … ; Look for people who will aim for the remarkable, who will not settle for the routine.' David Ogilvy

> 'A desk is a dangerous place from which to view the world.' John Le Carré

> 'Because a thing seems difficult for you, do not think it impossible for anyone to accomplish.' Marcus Aurelius

> 'If your actions inspire others to dream more, learn more, do more and become more, you are a leader.' John Quincy Adams

When you are the boss of other people, you have an added responsibility when trying to excel in your work – it is not just your own performance that you are trying to optimize, you are also responsible in part for helping your staff to succeed in their own work and careers.

By appropriately applying and practising all of the 50 secrets contained in this book, you can work well with anyone, including people who report to you. When you have staff looking to you for guidance and direction, it is essential that you lead by example and by 'walking your talk' – it is never wise to tell one of your staff how to act and to operate while doing the exact opposite yourself.

Working well with staff involves you mastering the skills of managing and leading people. In addition, when you have more than one person working under you, you will also need to learn the best ways to manage and lead a team. Much is written about the best ways to lead others and the following three strategies are the most important techniques that you should follow.

TURN A GROUP INTO A HIGH-PERFORMING TEAM

When you are given the task of managing a team, be ready to ensure that the group is genuinely a team of individuals who work well together. Too many teams are dysfunctional and are plagued with poor communication, lack of direction, selfishness and little sharing – they are teams only in name. To create a high-performing team, the key is to align all members of your team so that each member is moving in the same direction and understands their role and contribution. A good analogy is to think of a team of rowers where, if each rower is not totally aligned with all the other rowers, the boat might go round in circles or even capsize. Your task to is align any team that you are put in charge of. Such alignment can be based around shared mission and vision statements, team goals, mutual expectations and a common understanding of how tasks and activities will be carried out. Your staff should also be aligned around the kinds of behaviours and mindset you require. You can achieve this in the following ways:

- Decide on the aim(s) or goal(s) around which you wish to bring people together. It might be a shared sales goal, to understand your expectations, for you all to trust one another or to agree a new team mission statement.
- Bring your staff together as often as needed to both communicate well what you want them to understand and do and, more importantly, to listen well to them. The aim is to win over their hearts and minds and, in order to do this, you must be ready to help them understand why you need them to do certain things.
- Lead by example, being ready to demonstrate what you expect of others.

MOTIVATE AND RETAIN HIGH PERFORMERS

You can help yourself to excel by having staff who themselves are exceeding expectations and exhibiting high potential. When you have such talent reporting to you, you need to motivate them to want to continue performing well and to wish to continue working under you. Here are some tips for inspiring and retaining such key staff:

- Be a leader people want to work for and a person they trust. A key is communicating well and showing your team that you trust them.
- Reward your team fairly. This is not just a question of financial remuneration but also of giving your staff recognition, opportunities and promotions.
- Support your staff's career and life plans. This will be challenging for you when one of your high-performing team members wants to move on, either within your organization or elsewhere. Your first instinct might be to try to keep them but is that really in the best interests of the individual concerned?
- Create and maintain a positive and healthy work environment. You need your staff to be happy to come to work, to a place where there is little stress, anxiety or friction. This starts with you, so be someone who does not give others stress and anxiety.

In addition to these four tips, if you diligently follow all of the advice given in this book, you will always be able to attract, motivate and retain high-performing staff.

MANAGE POOR PERFORMERS

In an ideal world, you should hire and accept into your team only those who bring with them great experience and fantastic potential and who are strongly motivated. Sadly, this is rarely the case and, as a result, you may have to work with staff who are not performing well and/or do not have high potential to succeed in your team. Sometimes even someone who has been performing really well and shown great potential might start performing badly in their current role.

When you have staff who are not performing well, you have two options:

- Work with them to improve their performance, understanding that, as their boss, you are at least partly responsible for how each member of your team performs. Ensure that the individual concerned knows what they are supposed to do and why they should do it. In addition, help them understand how they should do their tasks, where they should be done and when.
- Have the courage to take them out of their role and remove them from your team. This can be achieved either by laying them off or encouraging them to find a more suitable job elsewhere. Ideally, only remove them from your team after you have tried seriously to improve their performance.

Putting it all together

When you have staff reporting to you, you have to focus on both your own performance and that of your team members. For you to succeed in your work, you will need to ensure that your team members also excel and that together you create a synergy where one plus one is greater than two. This is not easy and many first-time people managers struggle to take on this dual responsibility after having spent their working career focused only on their own performance. Many experienced leaders also struggle and, as mentioned at the start of the last chapter, bad bosses are a main reason for people choosing to resign and leave jobs.

This chapter covers a large topic and the three strategies were chosen as the optimal combination of three activities which can ensure that you succeed as a people manager. The key is to make sure your staff work together as an aligned team with commonly agreed goals and expectations. Far too many teams are dysfunctional and under-performing because they are poorly led, and team members might be stuck in an environment of poor behaviour and weak communication with a lack of common focus and goals.

In addition to creating a genuine team, to ensure that you excel as a people manager, you must learn to inspire and retain high-performing staff while helping any member who is struggling.

42

Value diversity in all its forms

> *'We all should know that diversity makes for a rich tapestry, and we must understand that all the threads of the tapestry are equal in value no matter what their color.'* Maya Angelou

> *'Diversity is not about how we differ. Diversity is about embracing one another's uniqueness.'* Ola Joseph

> *'Diversity: the art of thinking independently together.'* Malcolm Forbes

> *'It is not our differences that divide us. It is our inability to recognize, accept, and celebrate those differences.'* Audre Lorde

> *'There is nowhere you can go and only be with people who are like you. Give it up.'* Bernice Johnson Reagon

Diversity means many things to many people. To some it is all about ethnic and cultural diversity; to others is it about the male/female divide, about different-aged staff or different socio-economic backgrounds; to others it is all about variety of thought and opinions.

Imagine working in an organization where there was very little diversity, for example where:

- everyone was the same gender
- everybody studied engineering at the same university
- nobody was under 35 years of age.

If an organization with that make-up faced different challenges and problems, do you think that the staff would be able to produce superior solutions and ideas to an organization containing far more employee diversity? The answer, which studies confirm, is that more diverse groups of people easily produce a greater variety of ideas and solutions – what one person might miss another person spots.

The world is increasingly flat, with organizations having increasingly diverse workforces. We see many older staff delaying their retirements and staying in the workplace while we also see more women entering the workforce, particularly in countries where female participation in the workforce has historically been low. Successful people are able to work with all forms of diversity in the workplace. Having a woman boss for the first time, or a team member who is 30 years older than you or having colleagues from China – no matter what kind of diversity crosses your path, embrace it as a positive opportunity to work with someone whose thinking and habits might be quite different from your own and from what you are used to.

The following strategies are intended to encourage you to benefit from three common types of diversity in the workplace – different backgrounds, the male/female divide and age.

APPRECIATE AND ACCEPT DIFFERENT BACKGROUNDS

Each of us brings to the workplace a unique selection of strengths and weaknesses, with our personality and character being uniquely formed by our particular backgrounds and experiences.

We all come from varied backgrounds: some are born into a life of private schools and elite universities while others have come from rough neighbourhoods, struggled financially and may have left school at 16. Beware of judging people by how they speak, where they went to school or where they live. It is wise not to show off or act in a way which suggests that you are superior.

A common example is when someone has been to university and their colleagues have not. In this case, the one who is a graduate might act, often without even realizing it, as an intellectual show-off or snob. It might come across in the form of putting down other people's seemingly simple ideas and thoughts or treating somebody's question or comment as stupid. Likewise, if someone has colleagues who may seem to be from a more privileged background than them, they should not be put off or feel inferior.

If a colleague acts and makes comments that show that they are affected by coming from a background which might seem better or worse than others', I would suggest that you coach them not to need to feel different and not to let it show.

VALUE YOUNGER AS WELL AS OLDER COLLEAGUES

Do the following kinds of comments sound familiar?

- 'He acts so old-fashioned, hating any new ideas from his younger colleagues.'
- 'She is so young and naive, thinking that she knows more than I do about this topic.'
- 'What a dinosaur! She doesn't even understand why we want to use Facebook at work.'
- 'He has only just left college and is so impatient – already expecting a promotion and a new job title.'

No matter what your age, do not make biased comments and assumptions about colleagues who are older or younger than you are. The above comments might make you laugh and may seem harmless enough, but they reflect stereotypical and often biased thinking. I am a strong believer that maturity and wisdom do not always correlate well with age – I know of younger colleagues who seem so wise.

You can gain considerable benefits from what all your colleagues can offer you in terms of advice and support.

- Spend time with older colleagues listening to and learning from them. Ask them questions to proactively seek out their wisdom and knowledge. You could learn how to avoid many of the mistakes that they might have made.
- Value and appreciate the energy, eagerness and ambition of young colleagues. Observe and learn from them.

ENCOURAGE AND SUPPORT WOMEN TO 'LEAN IN'

I borrow the term 'lean in' from the title of the Chief Operating Officer (COO) of Facebook's recent book in which she encourages women to speak up more, be more assertive and be more present in the working world. I challenge you to be the colleague, male or female, who treats everyone in an equal and balanced way and who ensures that women's voices are heard as much as those of men.

As an example, in a meeting a woman may not speak up as freely or as confidently as her male colleagues and she may not persist in keeping her hand raised when someone calls for questions. Typically, when she does finally have a chance to speak, you may notice that others may not listen to her as closely as they listen to a man. She may even be cut off mid-sentence by a man who wants to speak. I call this a form of subtle discrimination which you should notice and counter. No matter whether you are a man or a woman, you might point out to a person chairing a meeting that a woman has her hand raised and wishes to speak. And, after a woman has spoken, you could acknowledge what she has shared and build on it with your own thoughts, rather than ignoring it and changing the subject.

Putting it all together

Diversity is a very popular business topic today, while the negative side of diversity – discrimination – remains a touchy and sensitive topic. Even in organizations which follow the letter of the law in terms of not discriminating against any individuals, it is common for people to show prejudice and bias. It might be as simple as avoiding speaking very often with certain colleagues – perhaps because of their age, sex, level of education, how they speak or simply the colour of their skin.

Have the courage to stand out from prejudiced colleagues by being open to and comfortable with all kinds of diversity among your colleagues and stakeholders. If you sense that someone is being ignored or marginalized, spend time with them and bring them into discussions, encouraging them to speak up as needed. This chapter's strategies cover three important areas of diversity – age, sex and background – but there are others, and the advice given in this chapter is easily adapted to any type of diversity and to ensuring that you help avoid or eliminate any potential discrimination in your workplace.

Some of your colleagues might make fun of you for suddenly appearing to act like a good Samaritan by giving time and supporting certain people (perhaps from a different background). Do what you know is the right thing to do. If you work with a boss or in a working culture which does not seem very tolerant of diversity and differences between people, you may reach the point when you decide to seek a new company to work for. Before making that final decision, try to lead by example and open up your colleagues and your boss to being more accepting and tolerant of diversity.

43 Actively seek feedback

'Feedback is the breakfast of champions.' Ken Blanchard

'Negative feedback is better than none. I would rather have a man hate me than overlook me.' Hugh Prather

'If you don't get feedback from your performers and your audience, you're going to be working in a vacuum.' Peter Maxwell Davies

'Ask for feedback from people with diverse backgrounds. Each one will tell you one useful thing.' Steve Jobs

'Everybody needs feedback, and it's a heck of a lot cheaper than paying a trainer.' Doug Lowenstein

How often does your boss or another colleague give you feedback about your performance at work? Have you ever asked your boss for feedback, for example after completing a particular task? Very few employees actively seek feedback and too many people do not wish to hear and learn from any feedback about themselves.

Feedback is other people sharing with you what they observe and experience when working with you. It can be sought from people on any aspect of you and your work – examples might include how you dress, your punctuality, your communication skills or your involvement in a project.

Most employees are given feedback during an annual performance evaluation discussion with their boss and this formal once-a-year event is the only feedback that some people ever receive. If you really want to excel, you need to know the areas of your work in which you are currently not excelling. For this you need to take a step further and seek feedback, not simply wait until the annual performance review time. Show those around you that you wish to develop and that you would really appreciate their insights and comments.

You will need to develop a bit of a thick skin and must not rush to react. Recognize that you have asked someone for feedback and what you want to know is what the other person honestly feels. Sometimes the truth hurts but, without hearing truths, how can you improve in your work?

SEEK SPONTANEOUS FEEDBACK

Get into the habit of asking colleagues for feedback about how you performed when you have just completed a particular task. The best feedback is the instantaneous kind where it is given as soon as something has happened. Examples might include someone giving you feedback about:

- a presentation that you have just completed
- a sales pitch that you have just finished
- a meeting that has just ended at which you were the meeting chair.

Such immediate feedback is good because the task will be fresh in your mind but also in the minds of those giving you feedback.

You may find that people are not used to being asked to give such spontaneous feedback and they may be hesitant at first to say very much, particularly for fear of sounding too critical and negative about your work. Encourage people to speak up and ask them to be as frank and honest as possible.

ASK OTHERS TO GIVE YOU 'FEEDFORWARD'

We cannot change the past but we can influence what happens in the future. Feedback describes what has already happened and there is a danger that it can get negative and critical. As an alternative, you could seek suggestions for how you can be more successful in the future. Such suggestions have been called 'feedforward' and having feedforward sessions with your boss or colleagues can be really helpful in enabling you to succeed.

In a feedforward session, think of areas in which you wish to improve. These could relate to any of your skills and behaviours. Share your goal with a colleague or small group of colleagues – for example, you might say, 'I wish to be a better listener'. Then ask them for suggestions on how you might achieve this goal – suggestions for the future, not feedback about the past. Listen carefully and take notes and say thank you. You could carry out this simple process several times, with different goals and involving other colleagues. In return, you might offer to give others feedforward in response to being told their goals.

Ideally, what you want is a combination of feedback and feedforward – feedback after you have completed a task or activity and feedforward when you are wishing to work on your behaviours, skills and future tasks. As a rule, I prefer giving colleagues feedforward rather than feedback for a number of reasons:

- It is more positive and motivating to help people to be 'right' than to show them that they were 'wrong'.
- You can give helpful feedforward without needing to know the person or their background and history.
- Feedforward is always positive; feedback tends towards the negative, which can be quite upsetting.

THANK PEOPLE FOR GIVING THEIR COMMENTS

Many people find giving others thoughtful feedback or feedforward very difficult because they have limited experience of doing it. In addition, giving someone honest feedback, particularly when it could be construed as negative, is not easy. It is important that you recognize the effort taken by those sharing with you by acknowledging and thanking them.

Putting it all together

Being able to give and to receive feedback are essential skills needed by anyone in the workplace. Without feedback, we risk working 'blind', without ever truly understanding how well we are doing and how we might improve our performance at work.

Nearly every large organization in the world has an annual performance evaluation process in which your boss, and perhaps others, will give you feedback on your performance. It is important to realize that relying on feedback being given only once a year is not good enough – you will not learn enough to enable you to excel in all areas of your work. Seek feedback all the time, whenever you have undertaken a task in which you would like to understand how well you did and how you could have done it better.

When you wish to develop your skills and behaviours in certain ways, try asking for 'feedforward' from your boss or colleagues to get suggestions from them on what you could do to become better or stronger. And always thank anyone who gives you feedback or feedforward – remember that it takes effort on their part.

44 Always manage your emotions

CC *'It's not what happens to you, but how you react to it that matters.'* Epictetus

CC *'Grant me the serenity to accept the things I cannot change, the courage to change the things I can, and the wisdom to know the difference.'* Reinhold Niebuhr

CC *'Speak when you are angry and you will make the best speech you will ever regret.'* Ambrose Bierce

CC *'Anger is only one letter short of danger.'* Anon.

CC *'Life is 10 per cent what happens to you and 90 per cent how you react to it.'* Charles R. Swindoll

If I asked your colleagues how emotional you are, how might they respond? Are you someone who easily becomes angry, happy, jealous or upset? When you are working, what might cause you to become emotional? Can you recall what has made you get angry, upset or jealous at work? Many people are not even aware of how and when their emotions change, and they might be surprised when someone asks a question such as: 'Why are you suddenly acting so upset?'

Emotions are the signs of how you are responding to things happening around you and they can be split into four types – sad, happy, anxious and angry. People show their emotions in different ways and it is often quite easy to see when someone is feeling strong emotions – for example, the angry person who turns red and raises his voice – although some people are good at hiding their emotions.

'Emotional intelligence', often referred to as EQ, is a measure of a person's understanding and control of their emotions. People with low EQ tend to exhibit a combination of little awareness and little control of their emotions – they tend to allow their emotions to control them rather than being the master of their emotions.

Negative emotions are often stirred up when events are not turning out as we had hoped or planned. We might be jealous because a colleague won an award which we had hoped to win or we might be upset and angry because our boss did not award a salary increase that we had been expecting.

Recognizing and managing your emotions are important skills at work.

FOOL OTHERS BUT NEVER FOOL YOURSELF

Always be honest with yourself about how you are feeling, no matter what kinds of emotion might be building up inside you. If you are:

- **jealous** of a colleague's success, admit that you are feeling jealous
- **hurt** that your boss has snubbed you, know that you are hurt
- **ecstatic** that a horrible colleague has been fired, admit that you feel happy
- **sad** that you were not chosen to head a new project team, recognize that you are upset.

Pretending to ourselves that we are not feeling something does not make that emotion disappear. Instead, it continues to build up inside us and, at some point, the pent-up emotions will become visible or somehow affect you, perhaps by making us ill. Admit to yourself what you are feeling and then decide how you are going to react. Most importantly, decide how (if at all) you would like others to know what you are feeling. Do you need to express your anger, upset, sadness, anxiety, jealousy?

MANAGE HOW YOU REACT

Some people seem to operate on autopilot and they immediately react when they become emotional. What triggers you to react in a potentially negative way at work?

Very emotional people often immediately show their emotions in ways which can be quite upsetting – shouting in the office, speaking rudely, walking around and waving their hands in the air. I have seen many angry and upset colleagues making their colleagues tremble and cry. How can anyone hope to excel in their work if they let themselves have such a negative impact on their work colleagues? Here are some tips on how to ensure that you never overreact when you are becoming emotional about something.

- Try not to say anything, and pause. Sit down if you are standing and, rather than speaking, simply count to ten in your head and breathe slowly.
- If the people around you expect you to say something, try a few words such as, 'Just give me a moment to collect my thoughts.'
- Be careful that tiredness, stress and overwork do not cause you to react more strongly than normal when something triggers your emotions. If you did not get a good night's sleep, recognize that this might make you more emotionally sensitive than usual and more liable to react when something happens. Also recognize how you react when colleagues are emotional and try not to let their emotions affect how you feel and act. If a colleague is very angry or upset, try to give that person space and leave their presence.

HELP OTHERS TO RECOGNIZE THEIR EMOTIONS

What do you say and how do you react when your boss, staff or colleagues become emotional in the office? Perhaps you have colleagues who easily get angry and then act in a mean way in the office? Or do you have a colleague who is very sensitive and becomes jealous and upset on a regular basis?

Normally, people like this need a helpful colleague to calm them down and remind them how they are appearing to others. The difficulty is that, when someone is emotional, they are often unwilling to listen to anyone else and, if you try helping them with words of advice and support, you might find yourself pushed away by that person and seen as a 'know-all' or nosy colleague. Use the skills of discernment and judgement which you honed in Chapter 25 to decide when to speak up and when to keep quiet. As a rule of thumb, put yourself in your colleague's situation and ask yourself if, with hindsight, you would have liked someone to give you some helpful comments and advice at that moment. If the answer is yes, then speak up.

Putting it all together

Remember that you are in charge of your emotions and it is you who:

- chooses to be upset when your colleague forgot to thank you in her presentation
- decides to be jealous because colleagues have been given new company cars
- opts to be sad and depressed because your job role has been reduced in size.

This chapter main's intention is to encourage you to control your emotional reactions. So many people lose their jobs because of how they interact with and around other people. Often they cannot see that they might be acting too emotionally. Only after they are told about their faults do they ask, 'I never knew that I reacted in that way when I was upset or angry; why did no one tell me earlier?' It is often too late after you have become very angry in the office or shown intense jealousy with your colleagues – you may have lost friends, reduced your chances of being promoted or, even worse, lost your job.

Be aware of your emotions and choose when and to whom you show them – there may be times when it is appropriate to tell or show someone that you are not happy about something, while at other times it may not help you to speak up at all.

Finally, be open to helping other people to manage their emotional reactions. You might save a colleague's career by intervening before they overreact.

Have the courage to risk failing

45

 *'He who risks and fails can be forgiven. He who never risks and never fails is a failure in his whole being.'* Paul Tillich

 *'The biggest risk is not taking any risk... in a world that's changing really quickly, the only strategy that is guaranteed to fail is not taking risks.'* Mark Zuckerberg

 *'Take calculated risks. That is quite different from being rash.'* George S. Patton

 *'It's fine to celebrate success but it is more important to heed the lessons of failure.'* Bill Gates

 *'The cave you fear to enter holds the treasure you seek.'* Joseph Campbell

A person's biggest work successes are often those based on decisions or actions that were filled with risk – decisions and actions that others might have been afraid to make for fear of failing. When is the last time you overcame fears of failing and took the plunge with a task or activity?

I have been a career coach for many years and I have met hundreds of people who want to change jobs, employers or professions but are too afraid to do so. I have also heard countless stories of people being afraid to take a step forward in different kinds of ways, such as:

- being afraid to confront their boss
- not wishing to call a potential client for fear of rejection

- holding back in a meeting from sharing an idea for fear of ridicule
- being afraid to question fraud in their company for fear of being fired.

What are we afraid of when we think that we might fail? Is it simply the embarrassment of not succeeding, the chance of being given a poor annual performance evaluation or the possibility of losing one's job? Each of us needs to find our own levels of risk tolerance, recognizing that some people are naturally more risk-averse or risk-seeking than others.

The key challenge is to recognize those critical moments when you need to decide whether you hold back or move forward, hoping for success but knowing that failure is a possibility. In these moments, you need to decide how important that success would be and what the chances and costs of failing are. Courage could be viewed as making an objective decision where you take calculated risks in return for some desired outcomes.

UNDERSTAND YOUR RELUCTANCE AND FEAR TO ACT

Explore what is really stopping you from getting started with a task. Ask yourself: 'Why am I afraid and reluctant to…?' You might respond that, if you fail, you might be fired or told off by your boss and made fun of by your colleagues. But how realistic are you being? Humans are very good at overplaying the negatives in life and we seem to create fears when reality time and again shows us that our fears are rarely justified. Many fears are irrational – they are like the child who is afraid of the dark in their own bedroom.

Even if you did not succeed at something, is your boss really going to fire you? Or tell you off? Does he not know what work and tasks you are embarking upon?

PRACTISE TAKING CALCULATED RISKS

What exactly are risks? Risks are the potential that something will be lost – it might be a client not being won, a product failing a quality test, a deadline missed or a proposal not accepted. A calculated risk is one where you would be able to accept the possible loss. In order to calculate the risks, they firstly need to be understood and acknowledged.

'No pain, no gain.' You might have heard this saying before. It is a simple reminder that risk is a trade-off – normally, the higher the possible gains from a particular action, the higher the level of risk. When you are contemplating doing something, you need to decide how important the potential gain or upside is. And can you accept the potential downside or loss? Ideally, the probability (or chance) of success should be high, particularly if the negative repercussions of not succeeding are also high.

It is not just a question of needing courage to do something. There may also be a cost of not acting in the first place and sometimes doing nothing is not an option, with the challenge being to minimize the potential risks of any choice you do make.

There will be times when you will have to use your intuition or gut feeling in order to make a final decision. This can be quite easy when the task is something that is in your area of expertise or comfort zone. The problem comes when you need to do something quite new. Often, in such cases you have no choice but to seek the advice and support of others, which is the subject of the next strategy.

SEEK ALLIANCES AND SUPPORT

It can be hard being courageous alone, particularly when you have nobody to sense-check the concerns and fears that are holding you back from acting. When we are alone at work, we can come to fear so many things and we often overestimate the degree to which other people are aware of and care about what we are doing.

If you need to do something but you are having doubts for fear of not succeeding, seek the help and support of your boss, colleagues or other stakeholders. Of course, there is a risk that those you ask might make a suggestion that you do not want to hear:

- 'What is delaying you? It is obvious that you should…'
- 'Are you crazy? Of course you shouldn't…'

So think how you will ask for input: 'It is important that I undertake this task and I want to chat with you about the possible downsides if I am not successful.' In this way you can focus on the potential risks with your colleague or boss, and not on whether or not you act.

There is a downside of being seen to rely upon others in this way: it may demonstrate that you are not very comfortable in taking initiative and responsibility, and will only act if you are doing what others think is right.

If you are working together in a team or group, you could discuss the task and the potential risks of failures as group issues. You could aim to reach a consensus decision or call for a show of hands.

Putting it all together

Getting started can be one of the hardest parts of undertaking many tasks and work responsibilities. Too many people like to procrastinate and delay jumping into things. So many examples of success start from people overcoming their fears of failure and starting tasks where they have taken calculated risks in the hope of some great success.

When you fear doing something, explore what it is that is holding you back and try to be as objective and as honest as possible. Take calculated risks that you can live with, avoiding tasks with a high chance of failure, or where failing would lead to you losing your job.

I know of no successful person who can claim that they have never failed in their working career. If you wish to excel, you will need to push yourself and that will mean taking risks. When a moment arrives when you do fail at something, be honest with yourself about what has happened and try to learn from those failures. It is much better to fail at something you have tried to do than to fail to try at all.

46 Be resilient and do not give up

 *'However long the night, the dawn will break.'* African proverb

 *'Most of the important things in the world have been accomplished by people who have kept on trying when there seemed to be no hope at all.'* Dale Carnegie

 *'That which does not kill us makes us stronger.'*
Friedrich Nietzsche

 *'Life's blows cannot break a person whose spirit is warmed at the fire of enthusiasm.'* Norman Vincent Peale

 *'I really wish I was less of a thinking man and more of a fool not afraid of rejection.'* Billy Joel

The previous chapter urged you to do what you need to do to succeed and to accept the risk that you might fail. This chapter builds on this by explaining to you that people who excel in the workplace do not give up if they fail first time at something which is important to do – they are highly likely to try again.

We all need to have the mindset of the inventor of the light bulb, Thomas Edison. He tried and failed hundreds of times to create a functioning light bulb: he did not give up after his fifth attempt, nor after his hundredth attempt, and he is reputed to have tried over one thousand designs or trials. Edison showed exceptional resilience in the face of repeated setbacks.

When was the last time that you persisted with an important task even in the face of delays, setbacks or outright failure? I once bought insurance from a salesman who must have tried selling to me at least ten times until I finally gave him time to explore what I might need. If he had called me only nine times, he would have completely failed.

Sometimes we might be put off, not by major failures or rejections, but by a variety of work issues – for example, someone ignoring our request for a meeting, falling foul of office politics, a boss who does not like us, our hard work and ideas not being accepted, a presentation which does not impress our audience. If the desired results or outcomes are important to achieve, then we must learn to keep going in spite of any obstacles that we face.

DO NOT TAKE IT PERSONALLY

Try never to take failure and rejection personally. Some people can become quite upset and depressed if they fail to achieve a desired result and they might think of themselves as being a poor performer, underachiever or someone not capable of success.

Maybe you did make a mistake, misunderstood the task or forgot how to do something – learn from this and move on, but do not beat yourself up. And remember that there might have been other reasons why you partly or wholly failed to achieve what you wanted, such as:

- the goal may have been unrealistic or too ambitious
- resources were not available
- certain factors were beyond your control.

The secret is to develop a habit of acknowledging what is happening and to want to learn from it, but not to become emotionally attached to what has happened. As soon as we let ourselves become emotional about something that has not gone well, we risk becoming irrational and overdramatic, saying things like:

- 'That's it, forget it. I'm not doing this again.'
- 'How embarrassing that we failed. I'm not bothering to try once more.'

Be thick-skinned when communicating with others who might make comments about you failing. I would suggest that you ignore people who seem to be enjoying your failure or saying things such as 'I told you so', 'I never thought you would succeed but you insisted on trying' or 'You've tried. Now let it go and move on.'

VIEW FAILURES AND REJECTIONS AS LEARNING TOOLS

The best way to learn something is from experience – to actually try doing the task or activity. Great learning can come when you face challenges and difficulties and when you might not succeed. The best learning takes place afterwards, when people review, discuss and analyse what has happened.

If something is very important to do or to achieve, and if you fail or are rejected in your first or even your third attempt, it would be foolish to try again without having tried to learn from what happened in the earlier attempt(s). Treat each failure as an opportunity to understand:

- what to avoid doing next time
- how to fine-tune the task to ensure success
- how to spot when things might be going awry.

Some tasks, such as creating a new product or design, may take multiple attempts and to succeed first time is unusual. In these cases each failed attempt is often viewed as an expected part of the development process and there is less stigma attached to failing. Contrast this with tasks where only one attempt is possible – bidding to win a contract, hiring a new employee or launching a new product – situations where failure is really not an option for an organization. In those cases it is so important not to fail that you need to prepare really well, understanding what you can learn from similar experiences in the past.

BE THE VOICE OF RESILIENCE ON YOUR TEAM

When you are part of a team that might be struggling to complete a piece of work, you can choose to take a role of being the encourager – encouraging the team to continue trying to succeed, motivating everyone not to give up too easily in the face of any difficulties or failures.

You could be a lone voice in your team if the rest of your colleagues have all pretty much decided to give up. If you feel that the team has to continue on a task, you need to decide how to inspire your team to 'dig deep' to continue. If you are the leader of the team, you might be able to use a combination of force (for example, we cannot go home until we have completed the task) as well as of positive encouragement. But, if you are simply a team member, you may have to rely upon your skills of persuasion and act as a 'leader without the job title'. It is very hard to encourage others to act with more resilience – even if they do agree to continue trying to do something, their hearts might not be in their work and they would literally do it 'half-heartedly'.

Putting it all together

So many people give up too easily and, as a result, they never achieve the level of work success that might otherwise have been possible. People might overcome any hesitation in trying out something once but, in the face of the first setback, rejection or failure, the majority of people do not continue and simply give up. It is impossible to excel in your job and career if you are part of this majority – you would be leaving the minority who would be persevering, trying again and in many cases eventually succeeding. Can you imagine how many other light bulb inventors tried, failed and gave up during the time that Thomas Edison was showing amazing resilience by trying again and again until he eventually succeeded?

Not giving up is in itself a form of excelling and can enable you to stand out among your colleagues. To ensure that you are able to maintain the resilience and persistence you need to understand and practise this chapter's three strategies, be ready to ignore the naysayers – colleagues who are happy to see you fail, who may be jealous that you are being persistent, and who may ridicule your failed attempts. So few people show great resilience and therefore you might find yourself alone as you do not let setbacks stop you. Learn from all your experiences and, most importantly, from those failed attempts and rejections – think what you can do better next time – remembering that each setback is one step closer to success. And, finally, be ready to help and encourage your colleagues or team to be resilient and not to give up trying.

47 Build your own unique brand

> **'For me, being memorable is more important than winning.'**
> Ricki Lake

> **'Create your own visual style... let it be unique for yourself and yet identifiable for others.'** Orson Welles

> **'In order to be irreplaceable one must always be different.'**
> Coco Chanel

> **'You were born to be an original. Don't die a copy.'** John Mason

> **'Your premium brand had better be delivering something special, or it's not going to get the business.'** Warren Buffett

Today, very few people can hope to stay with the same employer for the whole of their careers in what have been called 'jobs for life'. Instead, we see a working world where each of us may work with at least two and perhaps many more organizations over their working careers. In addition, increasing numbers of professionals are choosing to be self-employed, helping a wide array of clients.

In order to impress a new employer or new client quickly and genuinely, it is essential to be viewed as someone who stands out in your field of expertise or area of work. It is rather like a brand of food standing out on the shelves of a supermarket in such a way that it becomes the brand of choice for shoppers.

The ideal branding for someone wishing to excel at work should be one that would enable them to stand out, be memorable and potentially be a person who:

- the boss would turn to when needing a great job done
- stands out as the obvious successor to fill their boss's shoes
- is liked and admired throughout an organization
- is the person with whom a client would choose to work.

But what do we mean by 'branding'? It is the sum of all aspects of you and how these appear to others – when your senior colleagues are talking about your career potential, what they say about you and how they think of you can be called your branding.

The ideal branding is one that is unique and easily remembered for some individual and very positive reasons and that shows you in the best positive light. I coach for a global company whose CEO must sign off on all promotions above a certain grade level. He will not consider candidates for promotion unless he has heard something positive about them; otherwise he wonders why they would truly be worthy of being promoted. What this CEO is actually looking for is evidence of great personal branding from those members of staff who are hoping to grow in his organization.

CREATE A MEMORABLE AND UNIQUE MESSAGE

What strengths and other aspects of yourself do you want others to know about you? In other words, what would you like your branding message to focus on? It can cover all aspects of how you appear and perform in the workplace and might include:

- **skills and knowledge** that you want others to know that you possess – perhaps it is your great time management or your technical skills or perhaps you wish to be seen as an expert in a certain area
- **particular work experience** – which might include your negotiation experience or your ability to have solved complex manufacturing problems
- **aspects of your behaviour or mindset** – such as being really persistent, collaborative or a great team player

- **how you appear to others** – you might wish to project a very professional image in how you choose to dress or you might wish to be very individual in how you dress, for example by wearing a bow tie.

Ideally, your branding message is refined to suit your work environment and job role, with an eye on what might be required in order to be promoted or to grow your career in some other way. For example, if your company has begun focusing on the importance of change management and doing processes in new and optimal ways, then you might want your branding message to reflect your strengths in that area. Was there a notable recent example of you successfully helping colleagues to recognize a need for change and to work through it?

Part of developing a unique brand is for you to master the entire contents of this book and then to decide which secrets need your attention so that you optimize your unique set of offerings as an employee, colleague or boss in your workplace.

SEEK OUT VISIBILITY

How do you wish to communicate and make your branding message visible? You must ensure that all of your key strengths and attributes are visible to and recognized by the people who matter in your working life. Start by making a list of all those people who need to know and understand you. These might include colleagues, staff, suppliers, bosses, competitors and clients who together make up your stakeholders. Take your list and create a kind of marketing plan: determine who needs to know you better and for what reasons and then use this to map out how you will market yourself.

You should not market yourself in a superficial or showing-off kind of way. People rarely appreciate others who blatantly brag about themselves and who 'blow their own trumpet'. The secret to successfully marketing your strengths is through being subtle and diplomatic and also in giving others visibility. If you are part of a successful project management team, share your group's success by email, in conversation or in a company newsletter using 'we' more than 'I' when describing the success. You need to strike a balance by ensuring that your skills and contributions are visible without it appearing that you are being selfish.

COLLECT AND SHARE SUCCESS STORIES

This might seem like a small tip, but it has a surprising impact on how you would be perceived and known by others if you were to become a storyteller in your organization. By storyteller I mean that you might become someone who is willing to:

- write and share work and business success stories
- give talks and speeches to various stakeholders or at external events on topics relating to your organization's success.

You will be seen as altruistic in helping others to gain recognition. In addition, you can control the agenda or content and ensure, when appropriate, that your audience will see your positive contributions to any success that you write or talk about.

Putting it all together

Treating yourself like a product that needs a marketing plan might sound odd at first, but it is an unusually successful tactic for ensuring that others see and understand you in the best possible light. It also avoids comments such as:

- 'But I never knew you were good at that. If I had known, I could have considered you for that promotion opportunity.'
- 'You were part of the team that developed that great plan? If I had known, you could have helped present it to the boss.'

Decide what branding messages you wish to create for yourself – that combination of skills, experiences and success stories that you need others to know about you. You can then focus different parts of your branding with different stakeholders.

Some final advice: avoid the common mistake of intending to show others some of your skills and inadvertently showing them a weakness. I recently saw an ex-colleague who was keen to be seen as the hard-working and well-organized new member of his team. He also wished to be more visible by attending and speaking at corporate events. Unfortunately, he arrived conspicuously late for an event and missed a planned speaking slot. Thereafter, he was seen as someone who was 'all talk and no action' – he had inadvertently achieved the opposite branding impact to the one he had hoped for. We all have a mix of strengths and weaknesses and you do not have to hide all your weaknesses, but at least do not make them obvious to others.

48

Get a life outside work

> 'In all my years of counseling those near death, I've yet to hear anyone say they wished they had spent more time at the office.' Rabbi Kuschner

> 'Don't confuse having a career with having a life.' Hillary Clinton

> 'Oh, for God's sake... get a life, will you?' William Shatner

> 'Don't get so busy making a living that you forget to make a life.' Dolly Parton

> 'If you neglect to recharge a battery, it dies. And if you run full-speed ahead without stopping for water, you lose momentum to finish the race.' Oprah Winfrey

Are you one of those people who spends long hours at work, takes work home and will go to bed thinking about work issues and problems? Such a person is living to work and must find it hard to create quality time with family and friends and also to have time for non-work-related activities.

It is important to go to work refreshed and rested to enable your body and mind to cope with the six, eight or ten hours that you will spend at work. If your brain is always 'at work', including over the weekends and in the evenings, you may be waking up mentally exhausted and risk burning out.

When I am coaching, I always encourage people to have a good work–life balance. It is not just about wanting them to avoid overworking; it is intended to stop them having the common regret of those who are on their deathbed – that they spent too much of their life working and worrying about work. How can we try to succeed in our work and careers but avoid feeling that we might have failed to truly live a full life when we look back with hindsight in our old age?

Gain a perspective on how you wish to spend your time, particularly the time outside work, which is so important and can actually remind you of why you are working . Perhaps you are working to have a great family life, to fund your passion for sailing, to be able to help your spouse's own business start-up ideas or to give your children the best possible education. Having good reasons for going to work will help you commit to the extra effort required in trying to excel in your work.

It is also good to allow your non-work life to come into your work because this can bring more meaning into your job while also reinforcing those important non-work aspects of your life. For instance, you might involve your family when possible, perhaps at family fun days organized by your company.

🎲 DETERMINE WHAT IS MORE IMPORTANT THAN WORK

Make a list of those parts of your life that are more important to you than your work and career. You might choose to include such things as your family's well-being, your children's education, building a dream home, doing charity work and having a great retirement. Your list is unique to you and you should not feel guilty if it is very short. When you have read this book, you may add things to your list as a result of reflecting upon your work and its part in your life. Sometimes we forget what is important and often work seems to be the most important thing in our lives.

Take your list and look at each item on it. You need to decide in what ways you can ensure that your work can contribute to your achieving each of your non-work aims and goals. Examples might include maximizing your income opportunities at work to be able to achieve some goals of giving your family a large house, a private education and/or great holidays. Alternatively, it might be having work that involves being located in different countries to enable you to fulfil a lifelong ambition to see the world.

BRING NON-WORK LIFE TO YOUR WORKPLACE

Try not to allow your life to be separated in a very black and white way between work time and non-work time. But do not allow your working life to creep into your non-working portion of your day, for example by taking work home or on holiday. The healthy ideal is to do the opposite: allow elements of your non-work life to enter your work. Examples of this might include:

- taking your spouse with you when you go on a business trip so that you can enjoy time together when you are not in meetings
- organizing charity and voluntary events with your work colleagues – you might all spend an occasional Friday doing charity work together
- sports and recreational activities – finishing work early to have an inter-departmental football match or organizing a company barbecue for families.

LEAVE WORK PROBLEMS AT THE OFFICE

Do not take work home and, if you must, try to ensure that it does not become a habit. If you live alone, you may have nobody to remind you to rest and to switch off. If you live with family, you need to understand that they need your time, focus and attention.

Once you have arrived home, try to switch off – do not check your work emails on your smartphone or computer. Likewise, try not to take files and other reading materials home to read. I realize that you may occasionally have to break these rules, particularly if you are trying to excel through knowing more and being better prepared, but, again, don't let it become a habit.

The most important thing is to avoid taking bad energy and attitude home with you. If you find that you cannot avoid taking work home in the evenings, try ring-fencing your weekends as 'no work zones'! You might set a rule of absolutely no office work on Sundays, for example.

If you have a long commute to work, you might decide to treat such commuting time as work time. If you are driving, you might think through issues and make work-related hands-free phone calls. If you take a train, taxi or bus, you might choose to read and write reports, memos, spreadsheets and emails. For many people, their time spent commuting can be very productive given the lack of colleagues to disturb them.

Putting it all together

Too many people fail to heed Hillary Clinton's advice of not confusing having a career with having a life. They might choose to excel at work but do not concern themselves with trying to excel in other aspects of their lives. They live the mantra of 'living to work' and are very happy when attending parties where the main question asked is 'What do you do for living?', at which point they simply talk about their job while the stay-at-home mums or dads might feel worthless because they have no job to talk about.

Choose how you will strike your own balance between the working part of your life and the non-work goals and aspirations you also wish to make time for. Do not be a lemming and copy your workaholic and stressed-out colleagues who claim to be trying to excel at work. They are the ones who may never get home in time to put their young children to bed and who, only much later when they are going through divorce, might feel regret at having allowed their work life to swamp their family life.

Be aware of your non-work goals and aspirations, and find a comfortable way to combine the demands of your work with the rest of your life. Recognize when you are over-working and taking too much work home but also try to inject some life into your work so that your working life is not 'all work and no play'.

If you are still not convinced, think about this question: if you were suddenly on your deathbed, would you be happy with how you have been spending your time and the balance you have had between working in your job and the rest of your life?

Guide others on their career journeys

> 'Be kind, for everyone you meet is fighting a hard battle.' Plato

> 'Few people are mind readers. Let them know they matter.'
> Dr Chris Peterson

> 'The greatest good you can do for another is not just to share your riches but to reveal to him his own.' Benjamin Disraeli

> 'Mentoring is a brain to pick, an ear to listen, and a push in the right direction.' John Crosby

> 'We make a living by what we get, we make a life by what we give.' Winston Churchill

Even if you are able to excel in your work, many of those around you may not find achieving work success quite so easy. Earlier, in Chapter 10, I encouraged you to seek the support of mentors in helping you to excel in your own career. You can also act as a guide and mentor to help younger or less experienced colleagues in their own jobs and careers. And there may be times when a more senior colleague might welcome your advice and counsel on certain issues. You might start by buying them a copy of this book.

Mentoring is a combination of skills and you will find your own mentoring style as a result of your work experience, personality and work environment. Mentoring can include:

- **coaching** others by acting as a 'mirror', to enable people to ask themselves the right questions and find their own answers

- **career counselling** individuals – helping them to map out the career options open to them including exploring what kinds of career moves are possible within your organization
- **sharing examples** from your own work and career to encourage others not to repeat your mistakes but rather to copy your successes
- **introducing people** to others with specific skills or expertise when you may not be best equipped to help someone with a particular work concern or challenge.

Mentoring is more of an intention and mindset than a specific set of skills or processes, and it is never too late to start mentoring and helping others. Mentoring will make you popular with those you help and ought to put you in a good light within your organization. In effect, you are volunteering to share your own wisdom and expertise, which is something that is hard for others to criticize. Some might be jealous of your enthusiasm and desire to help others – but you cannot please everyone all the time!

SUPPORT THE CREATION OF A MENTORING PROGRAMME

Consider helping to create a mentoring programme in your company – it does not matter what your job role and profession are. Anyone can take a lead with a mentoring programme and typically you might focus on offering mentoring to younger colleagues in the same job functions.

A programme of this kind is normally a voluntary programme in which employees are asked to sign up as mentors who are then available to giving mentoring support in confidence to colleagues, normally those who are younger and less experienced. Being seen to be the creator of this idea will win you a lot of positive kudos and it would give you a chance to be known by a wide range of colleagues who otherwise may not know you.

Try to obtain some training in mentoring for the volunteer mentors, including yourself. The benefit to you is that you can be trained as a mentor, which brings credibility and gives you an extra skill to put on your CV. You might also consider becoming trained as a career adviser, executive coach or life coach. You would then be multi-skilled and able to provide a combination of mentoring and coaching to your colleagues. This would make you a much-valued colleague and someone to whom many people would start to turn for advice and a chat.

GIVE CAREER GUIDANCE TO YOUR GENERATION Y COLLEAGUES

Young colleagues, particularly the so-called Generation Y (those under 30 years of age), are normally very keen to be given help and guidance on how best to perform in their job roles and what might be the best plan for their careers. If you offer to give them support and advice, these young colleagues can become your work friends and allies and could later help you in many ways. Even if you are also in the so-called Generation Y age category, you can still provide help and guidance to your peers.

An additional benefit of supporting these newer colleagues might be that they are motivated to want to stay and to grow their careers within your organization rather than jumping between employers.

Another tried and tested idea is to take newly hired colleagues out for lunch; in the process you will make a new ally and work friend. When you meet with them, be ready to listen and understand their career story to date, their job anxieties and concerns and in what ways you might be able to help them.

You might also offer to allow newly hired young staff or even interns to spend time working with you, even when this might not be part of any planned induction programme. They might 'shadow' you for a few days, watching and learning what you do. You might be concerned that this could be time-consuming and frustrating but it will be time well invested – for you to succeed, you need to be known by people and also be seen as someone who wants to help others to excel in their own work and career.

GIVE CAREER TALKS TO COLLEAGUES AND POTENTIAL NEW STAFF

To help increase your visibility and enable you to help others, you might want to share your career and job experiences through giving talks and chairing discussions. You might offer to give a lunchtime talk on a career-related topic, which any interested colleagues are invited to attend.

Topics should be those which focus on the dilemmas and challenges that most people in your organization face, such as how to get noticed and be promoted, how to succeed in the matrix-reporting structure and how to shine in the company's culture and work environment.

You might also offer to help your human resources department colleagues by making yourself available to speak at careers fairs and at schools and colleges. Offer to give short and inspiring talks which will leave any audience enthused and excited about the possibility of joining and working in your organization. Once you start doing this, you will become a star in the eyes of your organization's HR and recruitment colleagues and your boss(es) will get to know, even if you do not tell them.

Putting it all together

I do hope that, having read this far, you would agree that you cannot genuinely claim to be excelling in your work if you are not actively trying to help other people to excel in their own careers. Develop an attitude of wishing to share your success tips and stories with others, knowing that in return you will win new work friends and allies who also may one day be able to help you. But do not help someone in the expectation of getting something in return – be selfless and help unconditionally. The young colleagues who receive your advice and counsel will doubtless speak highly of you, and that can only be a good thing, even if you see no obvious benefit.

Be creative in how you choose to mentor and help your colleagues, trying out different ideas and solutions to see how optimal they are within your organization's culture and also given your own personality. This chapter has shared a few ideas for you to explore, from a very visible mentoring programme, training mentors, focusing your time on helping the Generation Y colleagues through to giving career advice talks both internally and also at recruitment fairs and events. The essential ingredient is that you are willing to get into the habit of always being happy to give time to share your experiences and tips with your new and less experienced colleagues. You may also find that some of your senior colleagues – and even your boss – might seek your mentoring advice. That is a sign that you really are excelling in your work!

(50) Leave a legacy in your workplace

❝ *'The meaning of life is to find your gift. The purpose of life is to give it away.'* Pablo Picasso

❝ *'All good men and women must take responsibility to create legacies that will take the next generation to a level we could only imagine.'* Jim Rohn

❝ *'Carve your name on hearts, not tombstones. A legacy is etched into the minds of others and the stories they share about you.'* Shannon L. Alder

❝ *'The only thing you take with you when you're gone is what you leave behind.'* John Allston

❝ *'The greatest use of life is to spend it for something that will outlast it.'* William James

No one works for ever and even the best job in the world will come to an end at some point, if only because old age sets in. No matter whether you have been in your current role for a few months, a few years or many years, if you are leaving a job, how you would like to be remembered and what would you like to leave behind as your legacy?

It is not enough only to excel during your time at your work. To be able to look back on your working career with pride, you cannot simply retire, resign and move on from each of your job roles and employers without having ensured that you leave behind a positive legacy. A legacy in the workplace can take many forms, such as:

- having been an inspiring employee and excellent colleague
- ensuring that your successor in your job role has been coached and mentored by you to ensure success
- enabling your colleagues to take on your work efficiently through your having left them with clear guidelines and support
- taking away positive memories and only speaking highly of your past colleagues and employers
- departing in a positive and happy way, not leaving your remaining colleagues with bitter memories of you
- if you had been a people manager, leaving behind a trained, motivated and engaged group of former team members
- being available to support your ex-colleagues as needed after you have left the organization.

Not all departures from a job are voluntary or very positive. If you reach a point of really not enjoying your work and not performing well and you have tried working through the issues, then consider moving on – don't wait until your performance declines visibly and you are fired. Choosing to resign enables you to engineer a positive departure and you can leave with your head held high. This, in itself, is a way of leaving a positive legacy.

The best method of ensuring that you will leave a great legacy behind is to plan and to work on your legacy while you are still working. The following three strategies will show you ways in which you can do this.

GROOM A SUCCESSOR

Make sure that the individual who will replace you is fully prepared and ready to step into your shoes. How can you ensure that this happens? Firstly, you need to give your organization time to decide whether they need to fill the role that you will be vacating. You can create this time by letting your boss know as soon as possible about your intention to resign and to move on. Once you have formally announced your decision to resign or to retire, you should be willing to remain in your role for at least the duration of your contractual notice period.

Helping someone to succeed in your job role is not as simple as giving them your job description and showing them your workstation. You should also do the following:

- Make the person feel welcome and comfortable.
- Spend time sharing details about your role and experiences – not only the things you have done well but also those tasks in which you have struggled or may even have failed.
- Introduce them to all of your stakeholders – clients, colleagues, team members, suppliers, bosses, etc.
- If they are new to your organization, acquaint them with the office politics and working culture.

If your organization were to unexpectedly lay you off, you would probably be surprised and even very upset. In that situation the last thing on your mind might be helping your successor to take over your role successfully. But, even if you are fired from your job, try to leave with your head held high and to show that you valued your time with that organization. Do this by proactively offering to spend time handing over your duties to a chosen successor or to your boss and colleagues.

SHARE YOUR INFORMAL KNOWLEDGE BEFORE YOU LEAVE

When someone leaves, the main loss to an organization is the knowledge that the departing person has acquired. Such knowledge is that combination of acquired work experience and understanding of how to succeed in the role and organization, and it has both formal and informal components.

Formal knowledge is that information found in work procedure manuals and company handbooks and policies – it is knowledge that is not easily lost when one person leaves an organization. The challenge lies with informal knowledge, which could be viewed as the wisdom and insights built up by each of us in the workplace, and we take this with us when we leave.

Our informal knowledge is unique to each person and examples might include:

- understanding who to speak with to better understand what is happening or to gain informal approval for a new idea or proposal
- knowing how to ensure that certain factory machines work well when key spare parts are no longer available
- understanding the shortcuts for carrying out certain tasks in your organization
- being able to extract from an accounting software system information that is not readily available and not mentioned in the user manual.

During the days or weeks leading up to your departure from your organization, spend time willingly sharing information with your boss, colleagues and successor (if one has been chosen). You might choose to share your informal knowledge with your colleagues even when you have no intention of resigning. This could be a generous thing to do, but recognize that knowledge is power and you might decide to retain such knowledge to help you to stand out and be more important and valuable in your workplace. But, when you are leaving your job and organization and wish to leave a positive legacy, you have no reason to hold back from sharing your wisdom and knowledge.

DO GREAT THINGS THAT WILL BE REMEMBERED

A few months or years after you leave your workplace, you may not be remembered particularly as people change roles and leave the organization and new staff move in. You might have been forgotten but the legacy of your good work might remain. How might the results of your work remain long after you have left? Start by being someone who excels both in what you do and in trying to make a positive impact and difference in your workplace. Perhaps you were the one who:

- proposed building a new factory which is now your employer's main manufacturing arm

- won a new client who has now become one of your employer's key accounts
- started a mentoring programme which has now been introduced throughout your company.

Putting it all together

After you have spent time in a job role trying to succeed day in and day out, it is only logical that you would wish to succeed in the manner in which you leave your job and employer. Too many people leave their jobs, voluntarily or otherwise, and do so hastily, without giving much thought to ensuring that they leave in a helpful, productive and positive way.

Always ask yourself: 'How would I like to be remembered after I have left and moved on?' The aim of this chapter's secret is that you must choose to be remembered in ways that show you to have been a great colleague, boss or team member.

Helping your successor to take over your role and be able to excel as you did is an essential part of any legacy. Sharing all of your knowledge, experience and wisdom with your successor as well as with relevant colleagues and bosses is also important, and the most valuable pieces of information that you can share are what I called the informal knowledge, which will leave the organization with you if you do not share it before you go. Finally, spend your working days doing work which you are proud of and the beneficial results of which will remain long after you have left your job.

In this way you are not excelling just while you work but also in what you have left behind. Aim to leave legacies in your former workplaces which, in the words of George Fabricius, become lasting monuments:

'Death comes to all, but great achievements build a monument which shall endure until the sun grows cold.'

ABOUT THE AUTHOR

Nigel Cumberland (Fellow of both the ICPA and of the InstLM) is a qualified chartered accountant and the co-founder of the Silk Road Partnership, a leading global provider of executive coaching and leadership training solutions to some of the world's leading organizations. Having worked all over the world for over 25 years, Nigel really understands what it takes to succeed in workplaces in locations as diverse as Hong Kong, Budapest, Santiago, Shanghai and Dubai. Previously he worked as a multinational Finance Director with Coats plc and he has also run subsidiaries for leading recruitment firms such as Adecco. In addition, he co-created an award-winning recruitment firm in Hong Kong and China – later sold to Hays plc, the UK's largest recruitment group.

Discover the secrets behind greatness

For more information visit:
www.secretsguides.com